# Professional Ethics:
# A Revision Guide
# for the BPTC

# Professional Ethics: A Revision Guide for the BPTC

## Joanna Barr

First edition: 2016

ISBN-13: 9781534934320

ISBN-10: 1534934324

# TABLE OF CONTENTS

# INTRODUCTION

This Revision Guide is intended as a practical contribution to support students taking the Professional Ethics module, one of the most challenging subjects on the Bar Professional Training Course, which over half (54%) of the students of mainstream institutions failed at first sitting in 2015.

It provides a digested overview of the most relevant provisions of the second edition of the BSB Handbook and of the Guidance documents as well as tips for successfully answering the multiple choice questions (MCQs) and short answer questions (SAQs)

This Revision Guide comprehensively sets out the essential principles in force at the time of publication to assist BPTC students in gaining an in-depth understanding of the framework of ethical obligations of the legal practitioners. Practical examples of instances where obligations conflict with each other are included to allow students to bridge the gap between the principles and legal practice and consolidate their understanding of the BSB Handbook. It will support students to develop the skills to gain the maximum marks on each question and avoid fatal flaws in all the modules of the BPTC.

Although the BSB has confirmed that the MCQs on the BPTC's ethics exams will be discontinued from the new academic year, the challenges in responding to the proposed six SAQs remain as they were deemed to be the most difficult section to pass.

The information in this Handbook does not replace the need to consult the current edition of the BSB Handbook as well as the applicable Guidelines available through the BSB App to ensure that all the obligations prescribed therein are met.

Failure to adhere to the provisions can result in a finding of professional misconduct against the barrister concerned. Newly admitted practitioners may also find the Bar Council's Ethics Committee's Ethical Enquiries Service useful (available by email at: Ethics@BarCouncil.org.uk or by phone on: +44 (0) 20 7611 1307).

Students should also review the amendments to the syllabus published by the BSB throughout the year.

# A Guide to using this Book

This Revision Guide assumes that the reader has a law degree or a Graduate Diploma in Law.

In addition to familiarising yourself with this Revision Guide, the BSB Handbook and relevant Guidance documents, it is recommended that you pay particular attention to the text underlined throughout this Revision Guide which emphasises the applicable tests for each specific ethical principle. You must know these tests in order to score marks both in the MCQ and SAQ section.

Although you are not expected to cite cases or refer to specific Rules, Guidance and Outcomes numerically, you need to remember their principles and in particular the formulations of any test defined therein. You must also be able to refer to all the Core Duties by their relevant numerical denomination and cite them verbatim.

## Answering Multiple Choice Questions

The MCQ section is particularly tricky as knowledge of the substance is not enough to achieve the pass rate of 60%. The questions challenge your attention to details and your ability to identify relevant information in the question, with fact heavy narratives and double layered combinations of answers which make simple principles confusing to identify.

As such, you should allocate your time carefully to read and re-read each question before identifying the key words that affect the scenario. You should also pay particular attention to the questions which are often confusing due to the use of double negatives or which require you to identify the answer which is the "most accurate" implying there may be one or more accurate answers but that the correct answer is somewhat more complete than the other answers. For instance, "Barristers are usually personally responsible for their own conduct and for their professional work" is incorrect as the word usually implies there are exceptions, which is not the case.

Be particularly mindful of answers that include "must", "may", "should" and aim to test your knowledge of whether an action or reaction is mandatory, discretionary or recommended pursuant to the provisions of the Handbook. For instance, "You must confirm the terms of her instructions by email" would be an incorrect answer when considering the method by which to send information at the time of engagement since although email is permissible it is not the only permissible method.

You may be questioned on any practical dilemma faced in the course of legal practice. When in doubt, start by identifying the Core Duties applicable, the capacity in which the person is acting (Practising Barrister, Unregistered Barrister, pupil, tenant, manager, student) and the potential conflict between the duties. This will allow you to narrow down the principles applicable and tease out the correct answer.

## Answering Short Answer Questions

You need to pass both the MCQ and SAQ section in order to achieve an overall pass. Each of the three SAQs is divided into a number of sub-questions. The number of individual points that you are expected to include in an answer is indicated by the total number of marks.

There is no restriction, other than the time available for the exam, on how many different arguments or points you are permitted to make for each sub-question. However, since your time is precious you should remain concise. The number of marks indicated for each sub-question should serve as an indication of how much to elaborate each answer. Marks are not transferable between sub-questions and only full marks, and not half-marks, are used. You need to outline the relevant principles under the correct sub-question and to reiterate a point if relevant to more than one sub-question.

After reading the question carefully and identifying the relevant keywords, the first step in answering the question is to identify the relevant ethical issue and write out the Core Duty applicable as well as the relevant Rule. Pay particular attention to laying out the test accurately. As mentioned above you should do this for every sub-question.

Remember that compliance with the Rules may not necessarily be sufficient to comply with the obligations of the Core Duties. If there are no Rules covering a situation, refer to the relevant Core Duties and apply them. Only then can you refer to the facts outlined in each scenario and apply the principles and test you laid out to resolve the ethical issues. In doing so, engage with the facts as though you were advising a real client. Keep your answer practical. Some of the marks allotted to the question are earmarked for intelligent discussion of the facts and you will fail to score if your answer is theoretical in nature.

Where the answer requires a definitive yes or no, do take a position and explain your rationale. You will not score marks for sitting on the fence. As you may be aware some ethical principles remain grey areas depending on the circumstance and in those cases. Such situations are clearly indicated in this Revision Guide and, in those cases, irrespective of the course of action you recommend, you will be assigned marks if you laid out the principles accurately and discussed the facts in support of your conclusion. Answers should provide a detailed description of these as well as a comprehensive and clearly reasoned explanation in support of the resolution proposed.

Last but not least, whenever you conclude that a course of action amounts to a breach of duty, refer to the consequences of the breach as would be the case if giving a practical answer to a client. Remember that if in doubt about the application of a Core Duty or Rule, always recommend consulting a Senior Counsel in your Chambers, the BSB or the Bar Council helpline.

In order to obtain high or full marks you are advised to write in full sentences so as to evidence your knowledge and understanding of the issues involved and your evaluation of the correct ethical approach to adopt in the circumstances. This is particularly relevant for the test.

However, be mindful not to write huge paragraphs and spend too much time on one question, to answer all the sub-questions and to keep your handwriting legible.

While bullet point style answers should be avoided, if you are short on time, they can be used as long as you lay out the relevant principles, the correct test and the main facts you wish to refer to in such a way as to convince the examiner that the ethical issues have been understood.

Best of luck!

# List of Abbreviations

| | |
|---|---|
| BMIF | Bar Mutual Indemnity Fund |
| BPTC | Bar Professional Training Course |
| BSB | Bar Standards Board |
| CAEF | Criminal Advocacy Evaluation Form |
| CD | Core Duty/Core Duties |
| CILEx | Chartered Institute of Legal Executives |
| CPD | Continuing Professional Development |
| FCA | Financial Conduct Authority |
| Handbook | BSB Handbook |
| HOFA | Head of Finance and Administration |
| HOLP | Head of Legal Practice |
| LLP | Limited Liability Partnership |
| LSA | Legal Services Act |
| LSB | Legal Services Board |
| PDA | Personal Digital Assistant |
| QC | Queen's Counsel |
| QASA | Quality Assurance Scheme for Advocates |
| SRA | Solicitors Regulation Authority |

# CHAPTER 1

## THE HANDBOOK AND THE CORE DUTIES

## 1.1 What is the Handbook?

The Handbook sets out the standards that BSB regulated individuals need to comply with. It is also a useful reference tool for consumers of legal services regulated by the BSB.

### 1.1.1 How is the Handbook structured?

The Handbook is divided into 6 parts:

- Part 1 is essential to understand when and to whom to apply the Handbook. Although it is a short section, when read together with Part 6 on the Definition section, it provides the basic knowledge you need to apply the Core Duties, Rules and Guidance.
- Part 2 covers the basic principles. While you do not need to cite the number of the Outcomes, Rules and Guidance when referring to them in the BPTC exam, you need to know the CDs verbatim and their numerical denominations. Learning them early on will help a great deal throughout the year and thereafter in your legal practice.
- Part 3 concerns the scope of practice and authorisation Rules and is particularly relevant for defining the scope of activities which the BSB authorised persons are permitted to conduct.

- Part 4 concerns the qualifications Rules that are relevant to gain practical knowledge of the Handbook in action.
- Part 5 is about the enforcement regulations and the consequences of failing to act in accordance with the Handbook.
- Part 6 contains the definition section that explains important terms essential to your understanding of the Handbook.

The Handbook does not, on its own, contain all the principles and obligations applicable. The Handbook is supplemented by the guidelines which also contain important enforceable obligations and are examinable for the BPTC examination:

- Guidance for Unregistered Barristers;
- Public Access Guidance for Barristers;
- Guidance on the Administration of a Barrister's Practice: namely Complaints Handling, Referral and Marketing Arrangements, Confidentiality, Self-Employed Practice (investigating, collecting evidence and attendance at police stations);
- Guidance on Professional Conduct: namely Reporting Serious Misconduct, Media Comment Guidance, Insurance and Limitation of Liability Guidance and Guidance on Clash of Hearing Dates;
- BSB Handbook Equality Rules; and
- BSB CPD Guide.

In relation to the issue of coming into possession of privileged information, the following cases are relevant:

- *English & American Insurance Co. Ltd & Others v. Herbert Smith* ChD 1987; (1987) NLJ 148; and
- *Ablitt v. Mills & Reeve (A Firm) and Another* ChD The Times 24 October 1995.

You should also review the following Crown Prosecution Service (CPS) Documents:

- The Farquharson Guidelines; and
- The Code for Crown Prosecutors.

The Chancery Bar Association Guidance on Money Laundering is also relevant.

## 1.1.2 Who does the Handbook apply to?

The Handbook applies to:

a) All barristers including:
- *Practising Barristers* - defined as barrister supplying legal service <u>and</u> holding practising certificate;
- Barristers undertaking the first non-practising six months of pupillage <u>or</u> second practising six months <u>and</u> registered with the BSB as *pupil*; and
- All other barristers who do not hold a practicing certificate but who have been called to the Bar by one of the Inns of Court and have not ceased to be a member of the Bar – referred to as *Unregistered Barristers.*
  Where the pupil is the pupil of an employed barrister (non-authorised body); of a manager or employee of a BSB authorised body or of an authorised (non-BSB) body; or undertaking external training with a BSB authorised body or an authorised (non-BSB) body, the obligations of the pupil will be those of an employee of the barrister's employer or the body concerned i.e. the obligations of an authorised (non-BSB) individuals.
b) *EU lawyers registered by the Bar Council* and by an Inn in connection with their practice in England and Wales.
  The obligations of the Handbook apply to them <u>only</u> in connection with professional work undertaken by registered EU lawyers in England and Wales.
c) *BSB authorised bodies,* their owners and managers referred to as *BSB regulated managers* or *BSB regulated owners* respectively;

d) Employees of a BSB authorised person – referred to as *authorised (non-BSB) individuals* who are <u>directly or indirectly</u> employed by a *BSB authorised person* and authorised to provide reserved legal activities by another *Approved Regulator*. It is to be noted that the only provisions applicable to authorised (non-BSB) individuals are the disqualification provisions.

e) Students and approved training organisations.
It is useful to note that the only part of the Handbook applicable to students and training organisations is Part 4 relating to the qualification Rules; and

The exception to this Rule is that for barristers, pupils, European barristers who work for a solicitor, a LLP or another body which has its own regulatory Rules under an Approved Regulator <u>and</u> are also regulated by the BSB, in case of <u>conflicting provisions</u>, the Handbook does not apply. The barrister, pupil or European barrister will be required to comply with the requirements of that other Approved Regulator and, will not be considered to be in breach of the relevant provision of this Handbook.

For the purpose of understanding the application of the Handbook you should know that the *BSB regulated persons* are:

a) barristers (i.e. Practising, Unregistered and pupils);
b) registered European lawyers;
c) BSB authorised bodies;
d) authorised (non-BSB) individuals; and
e) BSB regulated managers.

BSB regulated persons are regulated by the BSB whether or not their authorisation is suspended. Students and approved training organisations are not considered as BSB regulated persons as the Handbook only applies partially to them in relation to qualification provisions.

### 1.1.3 What are the obligations under the Handbook?

The Handbook prescribes a hierarchy of norms including the Core Duties, the Outcomes, the Rules and the Guidance that are applicable when addressing each situation.

#### 1.1.3.1 The Core Duties

The Core Duties (CDs) are the <u>mandatory</u> standards that all BSB regulated persons are required to meet. They define the <u>core elements of professional conduct</u>.

Disciplinary proceedings may be taken against a BSB regulated person if the Bar Standards Board believes there has been a breach by that person of the Core Duties set out in the Handbook <u>and</u> that such action would be in accordance with the Enforcement Policy.

There are 10 core Duties (CDs):

CD1 You must observe your duty to the Court in the administration of justice

CD2 You must act in the best interests of each client

CD3 You must act with honesty and integrity

CD4 You must maintain your independence

CD5 You must not behave in a way which is likely to diminish the trust and confidence which the public places in you or in the profession

CD6 You must keep the affairs of each client confidential

CD7 You must provide a competent standard of work and service to each client

CD8 You must not discriminate unlawfully against any person

CD9 You must be open and co-operative with your regulators

CD10 You must take reasonable steps to manage your practice, or carry out your role within your practice, competently and in such a way as to achieve compliance with your legal and regulatory obligations

### 1.1.3.1.1 When do the CDs apply?

Although all the CDs must be complied with, some CDs override others and some apply in particular circumstances while others apply at all times. The hierarchy of the CDs and their application will be explored in the following Chapters.

a) CD 1 overrides any other Core Duty in case of inconsistency;
b) CD 2 – the duty to act in the best interest of each client is subject to the following CDs:
   - CD 1 – duty to the Court;
   - CD3 – duty to act with honesty and integrity;
   - CD4 – duty to maintain independence; and
   - CD 8 – duty not to discriminate unlawfully against any person.
c) CDs 5 applies at all times, in all matters of private and professional life – duty not to behave in a way which is likely to diminish the trust and confidence which the public places in you or in the profession; and
d) CD 9 applies at all times, in all matters of private and professional life – duty to be open and co-operative with your regulators

Where a conflict arises between one or more CDs, the Rules and Guidance prescribe the course of action to follow in order to comply with the obligations laid out in the Handbook and Guidance documents.

The CDs should <u>at all-time</u> be read together with the Rules, Outcomes and Guidance.

### 1.1.3.2 What are the Rules?

The Rules located in Part 2 of the Handbook supplement the CDs, and are <u>mandatory.</u> In situations where specific Rules do apply, it is still necessary to consider the CDs, since <u>compliance with the Rules alone will not necessarily be sufficient to comply with the CDs.</u>

It is also important to note that the Rules provided in the Handbook are not exhaustive. In any situation where no specific Rule applies, reference should be made to the CDs.

The following Rules apply to both practising and Unregistered Barristers <u>at all times</u>:

a) Rule C8 - duty not to do anything which could be seen to undermine honesty, integrity and independence;
b) Rule C16 – duty to the client is subject to the duty to the Court and to the obligations to act with honesty and integrity and maintain independence;
c) Rule C64 to 70– <u>must</u> provide all information to the BSB as may require and comply with any decision of the BSB; must report some matters relating to disqualification to the BSB, must report serious misconduct of others and must permit the BSB <u>reasonable access</u> to inspect premises or documents.

### 1.1.3.3  What are the Guidance provisions?

The Guidance provisions are not mandatory but rather <u>assist in the interpretation and application</u> of the CD or Rules to which such Guidance relates by:

a) Providing examples of the types of conduct or behaviour that the Rules are intended to encourage, which would likely indicate or which may constitute non-compliance;

b) Explaining how the Rules apply to a particular type of BSB regulated person; and

c) Acting as a signpost to other Rules or to guidance on the BSB website or elsewhere which may be relevant.

### 1.1.3.4  What are the Outcomes?

The Outcomes are the <u>aims derived from the regulatory objectives</u> of the BSB and explain the reasons for the regulatory schemes and what it aims to achieve. Although they are <u>not mandatory</u>, they should be kept in mind when considering how the Core Duties and Rules (as appropriate) should be applied in particular circumstances.

The Outcomes will also be considered by the BSB in determining whether the obligations in a CD or Rule have been breached.

### 1.1.3.5  What are the Regulations?

The Regulations <u>bind the BSB</u> when considering whether a breach has taken place or whether actions should be taken.

### 1.1.3.6  What to do in case of uncertainty on the Rules applicable?

If the Handbook is silent on the ethical course of action to follow in case of a particular situation or there is any doubt, it is recommended that:

a) A Senior member of Chambers be consulted; and/or
b) The Bar Council's Ethics Committee's Ethical Enquiries Service be contacted by email at: Ethics@BarCouncil.org.uk or by phone on: +44 (0) 20 7611 1307.

## 1.2 What is the Bar Council?

The Bar Council represents barristers in England and Wales. Its role is to promote and improve the services and functions of the Bar, and to represent the interests of the Bar on all matters relating to the profession, whether trade union, disciplinary, public interest or in any way affecting the administration of justice.

It acts as the approved regulator of the Bar and it discharges its regulatory functions through the independent BSB.

## 1.3 What is the Bar Standards Board?

The Bar Standards Board is the <u>independent regulatory body</u> which regulates barristers and their professional practice and specialised legal services businesses in England and Wales in the public interest.

The BSB performs the following functions in accordance with the LSA and other statutes:

- Setting the education and training requirements for becoming a barrister;
- Setting continuing training requirements to ensure that barristers' skills are maintained throughout their careers;
- Setting standards of conduct for barristers;
- Authorising organisations that focus on advocacy, litigation, and specialist legal advice;
- Monitoring the service provided by barristers and the organisations we authorise to assure quality; and

- Handling complaints against barristers and the organisations we authorise and taking disciplinary or other action where appropriate.

The BSB's regulatory objectives are to:

- protect and promote the Constitutional principles, public interest and the interest of consumers;
- improve access to justice and public understanding of citizen's legal rights and duties;
- encourage an independent, strong, diverse and effective legal profession as well as competition;
- promote and maintain adherence to professional principles including:
  - the duty to the Court (CD 1)
  - the duty to act in the best interest of each client (CD 2)
  - the duty to act with honesty and integrity (CD3)
  - the duty to maintain independence (CD 4)
  - the duty to keep affairs of the client confidential (CD6)
  - the duty to provide competent standard of work (CD 7)

# CHAPTER 2

THE OBLIGATIONS OF PRACTICING BARRISTERS,
UNREGISTERED BARRISTERS AND PUPILS

## 2.1  The difference between Practicing and Unregistered Barristers

The Handbook defines a Practising Barrister as a barrister who is <u>supplying legal services and holds a practising certificate</u>.

Barristers who do not have a practising certificate either by choice or because they do not qualify for a practising certificate are called "Unregistered Barristers" because they are not on the public register of barristers who have practising certificates.

This chapter will explore the differences in the activities which the Practising and Unregistered Barristers are authorised to undertake respectively as well as the differences in the regulatory safeguards that would apply to each of them.

## 2.2  Types of legal services

### 2.2.1  Legal services

Legal services includes:

a) legal advice representation;
b) drafting; and
c) settling any statement of case witness statement affidavit or other legal document.

Legal services, other than reserved legal activities, can be supplied by anyone and are not subject to any special statutory regulation. This means that both Unregistered and Practising Barristers can carry it out with as only difference, this is, the prohibition against holding out as a barrister for Unregistered Barristers.

Barristers with practising certificates are subject to additional requirements for their practise such as having professional indemnity insurance and keeping their professional knowledge up-to-date, which do not apply to Unregistered Barristers. The clients of Practising Barristers also have access to complaints mechanism such as the Legal Ombudsman, safeguards which are not in place for Unregistered Barristers.

As such the Rules against holding out are intended to minimise the risks for clients.

## 2.2.2 Reserved legal services

Reserved legal activities are the legal services which can only be provided by those authorised to do so under the Legal Services Act. These include:

a) the exercise of a right of audience;
b) the conduct of litigation;
c) reserved instrument activities;
d) probate activities;
e) notarial activities; and
f) the administration of oaths.

It is important to note that <u>advocacy is not a reserved legal activity</u> unless <u>it involves the exercise of a right of audience</u>. As such, advocacy before an arbitrator or other tribunal where rights of audience are not required is not a reserved legal activity.

<u>Only Practising Barristers can provide reserved legal activities. Unregistered</u> <u>Barristers are not permitted to carry out these services.</u> It is a criminal offence to carry out a reserved legal activity without a practising certificate according to the Legal Services Act 2007 that has as punishment upon conviction of imprisonment for up to 2 years and/or a fine.

Barristers can also be authorised to carry out reserved legal services by another approved Regulator such as:

a) the Law Society (acting by the Solicitors Regulation Authority),
b) the Chartered Institute of Legal Executives,
c) the Chartered Institute of Patent Agents and
d) the Institute of Trade Mark Attorneys.

In that case they <u>must</u> not practise as a barrister and are not eligible for a practising certificate however, they may hold themselves out as a barrister and <u>must</u> inform the client <u>clearly in writing at the earliest opportunity</u> that they are not practising as barrister or registered European lawyer.

## 2.2.3 Non legal activities

It is important to note that the following activities are not considered to be legal services and as such can be carried out by any barrister whether practising or not:

a) sitting as a Judge or arbitrator or acting as a mediator, early neutral evaluation, expert determination and adjudications;
b) lecturing in or teaching law or writing or editing law books articles or reports;

c) examining newspapers, periodicals, books, scripts and other publications for libel, breach of copyright, contempt of Court and the like;
d) communicating to or in the press or other media;
e) giving advice on legal matters free to a <u>friend or relative</u> or acting as <u>unpaid or honorary</u> legal adviser to any <u>charitable</u> institution;
f) in relation to a barrister who is a non-executive director of a company or a trustee or governor of a charitable institution or private trust, giving to the other directors trustees or governors the benefit of his/her learning and experience on matters of general legal principle applicable to the affairs of the company institution or trust.

## 2.2.4 Pro bono legal activities

Self-employed barristers may provide pro bono legal services through a Legal Advice Centre but only those who are Public Access registered can provide pro bono legal services directly to the public.

Employed barristers on the other hand can provide legal services directly to the public only where the services are pro bono.

Unregistered Barristers who do not hold practising certificates (including first six pupils) are permitted to provide free legal advice to clients of a legal advice centre, providing they do not hold themselves out as barristers and do not undertake or offer to undertake any reserved legal services.

The only requirement to bear in mind is that the barrister must ensure that the professional indemnity insurance covers the pro bono services.

It is important to note that these Rules do not entitle someone who is not authorised to undertake reserved legal activities to carry them out pro bono and that giving free advice to a friend or as honorary legal adviser to a charitable institution is not considered to be legal services and as such can be undertaken by anyone.

## 2.3 Obligations when providing various types of legal services

Various obligations apply to various BSB regulated persons depending on the type of services provided.

a)  Non legal services

Whether a practising or Unregistered Barrister is providing legal activities or not, the Core Duties 5 and 9 apply <u>at all times both in private and professional life</u>. As such they apply when conducting non legal activities.

b)  Legal services

Whether for a Practising or Unregistered Barrister, when providing legal services all the Core Duties in the Handbook apply. The next section considers the additional obligations of Unregistered Barristers.

c)  Reserved legal activities

Practising Barristers and individuals authorised by other approved regulators are the only ones authorised to undertake reserved legal activities and are subject to all the Core Duties when providing such services.

However, in the case of individuals regulated by other approved Regulators, you will remember that if there are <u>conflicting provisions</u>, the Handbook does not apply. The individual will be required to comply with the requirements of that other Approved Regulator and, will not be considered to be in breach of the relevant provision of this Handbook.

## 2.4 Additional obligations of Unregistered Barristers

### 2.4.1 Additional obligations which apply to Unregistered Barristers at all times

CDs 5 and 9 apply to Unregistered Barristers at all times.

In addition to the applicable CDs when undertaking each type of legal activity listed above, the following Rules apply to Unregistered Barristers at all times:

a) Rule C8 - duty not to do anything which could be seen to undermine honesty, integrity and independence;

b) Rule C16 – duty to the client is subject to the duty to the Court and to the obligations to act with honesty and integrity and maintain independence;

c) Rule C64 to 70 – must provide all information to the BSB as may require and comply with any decision of the BSB; must report some matters relating to disqualification to the BSB, must report serious misconduct of others and must permit the BSB reasonable access to inspect premises or documents.

### 2.4.2 Additional obligation when supplying legal services

When supplying legal services, the Unregistered Barristers are subject to all the CDs. In addition, the following Rules apply:

a) Rule C3.5 – must ensure that ability to act independently is not compromised;

b) Rule C4 – duty act in the best interest of each client is subject to the duty to the Court; and

c) Rule C19 – if supplying or offering to supply legal services you must not mislead or cause or permit to be misled any client about:

- The nature and scope of legal services;
- Terms under which they will be supplied (who will carry out the work and the basis of charging);
- Who is legally responsible for the provision of the service;
- Whether entitled to supply these services and extent to which the provider is regulated;
- The extent to which you are covered by insurance.

### 2.4.3 Additional obligation not to mislead when supplying legal services

In addition, Unregistered Barristers are subject to an obligation not to mislead regarding their status <u>when providing legal services</u> (referred to as "holding out as a barrister") and this includes an obligation to provide information to clients.

The restriction on 'holding out' prevents barristers who do not have a practising certificate (unregistered barristers) but who are <u>supplying or offering to supply legal services</u> from using the title 'barrister' or otherwise conveying the impression that they are practising as barristers.

The fundamental principle is that one <u>must</u> not mislead or <u>allow anyone else to mislead</u> any person to whom he/she or his/her employer supply or offer to supply legal services. It is important to note that an Unregistered Barrister is responsible for his/her employer's acts if they are misleading in this context and failure to comply would amount to a breach of CD 3 and 4 and possibly 5.

Describing oneself as a barrister or conveying the impression that one is a barrister whether deliberately or not can happen in a variety of circumstances.

An individual who has been called to the Bar, can describe himself as a barrister if it is not in connection with the supply of legal services. He/

she can use the title "barrister" in a curriculum vitae for instance when not providing legal services. There may also be occasions on which it is unavoidable for barristers without practising certificates who are supplying or offering to supply legal services to disclose that they are qualified as barristers as for instance in job applications or enquiries by clients as to the barrister's background. In these cases there is no objection to indicating that you have qualified as a barrister but it should be made clear that you are not practising as a barrister.

When supplying or offering to supply legal services it is important that neither the Unregistered Barrister nor his/her employer use the title barrister, Unregistered Barrister or non-practising barrister. The following would be considered as holding out as a barrister:

a) Describing oneself as a barrister to clients, prospective clients, opposing parties or their representatives (included in any printed material used in connection with the provision of legal services such as on a card or letterhead, or on premises);
b) Using other descriptions such as membership of an Inn of Court which imply that the individual is a barrister in connection with supplying or offering to supply legal services.

This would apply particularly where an Unregistered Barrister is providing legal services to the same people to whom he/she provides "non-legal" services.

When providing legal services, Unregistered Barristers can instead use the titles "lawyer" or "legal adviser".

If you are self-employed, or work for an unregulated employer supplying legal services to the public, you should not use the title "Counsel", wear robes, or sit in a place reserved for Counsel, in Court. However, if you provide legal services only to your employer you may use titles commonly used in companies, such as in-house legal counsel, general counsel, and corporate counsel. You may also use the description "of Counsel" if you work for an employer which is an authorised person under the Legal Services Act.

It is important to note that describing oneself to clients or prospective clients as a non-Practising Barrister or barrister-at-law, titles which were allowed to be used in the past, is now also considered as holding out as a barrister.

There is however an exception for Queen's Counsels (QCs) who may continue to use the title even if they no longer have a practising certificate, but if they are no longer providing legal services, they must explain that they are not practising as a barrister.

A BVC or BPTC graduate can refer to themselves as a BVC/BPTC graduate and mention that he/she is a holder of this qualification.

## 2.4.4 Additional obligation to provide information

The obligation not to mislead includes an obligation to provide clear information to inexperienced clients about:

- their status;
- the extent to which they are regulated;
- the services supplied; and
- their insurance cover.

This is the case in particular where Unregistered Barristers are acting for inexperienced clients. Inexperienced clients are defined as including individuals and small organisations that would be entitled under the Legal Ombudsman Scheme Rules to make a complaint to the Legal Ombudsman if you were a practising barrister.

However, other clients, for example slightly larger organisations which only occasionally require legal services, may also be inexperienced. If there is any doubt as to whether your client has sufficient experience to understand the implications of instructing an Unregistered Barrister instead of a Practising Barrister, they must be given a written statement explaining:

a) that the barrister in question is not a Practising Barrister;
b) that he/she is not subject to certain Conduct Rules applying to practising barristers and the Bar Standards Board cannot consider complaints against them in relation to these Rules but only in relation to the Rules which do apply to Unregistered Barristers;
c) that the client has no right to complain to the Legal Ombudsman otherwise available for Practising Barristers;
d) that if the Unregistered Barrister cannot resolve any complaints himself/herself, the clients can complain to the Bar Standards Board and it will investigate any breaches;
e) whether he/she is covered by professional indemnity insurance which is not compulsory but strongly recommended.

In considering whether a company is inexperienced client it is the client that matters and not for instance the director or shareholder of the company. For instance if the director of a micro enterprise approaches you, the client is the micro enterprise which would qualify as an inexperienced client.

The client must also confirm in writing that they have received this explanation.

It must be noted that where an Unregistered Barrister is supplying services as an employees of a firm of solicitors or, a body subject to regulations by a professional body, the obligations to explain to the client about your status does not apply.

### 2.4.5  Additional obligation when acting pro bono

These requirements do not apply to legal services provided when working for a Legal Advice Centre. Unregistered Barristers who do not hold practising certificates (including first six pupils) are permitted to provide free legal advice to clients of a legal advice centre, providing they do not hold themselves out as barristers and do not undertake or offer to undertake any reserved legal services

## 2.5 What activities can a Pupil undertake?

Pupillages are divided between the first and second six. During the first six, since the pupil does not have a practising certificate, he/she cannot supply legal services as a Practising Barrister but can accept a <u>noting brief</u> <u>with permission</u> of his/her pupil supervisor or Head of Chambers.

They may describe themselves as a pupil barrister in that capacity in the context of supplying reserved legal activities. However, if they provide non legal activities or unreserved legal services in any other capacity, they should not describe themselves as a barrister or a pupil barrister and should follow the Rules and guidance for unregistered barristers.

During the second six, the pupils are granted a provisional practising certificate and may then provide legal services in accordance with Rule S19. They may refer to themselves as pupil barrister and should ensure that the client understands their status.

It is important that pupils do not hold themselves as member of Chambers or permit their names to appear as such as this would amount to a breach of CD 3, 4 and possibly 5. You should at all times ensure that the client understands your status.

## 2.6 Other specially regulated activities

In order to perform some specific activities you must comply with the specific training requirements of the BSB.

## 2.6.1 Police Station Attendance

While the previous ban on attending police stations has been removed, barristers should not attend a police station to advise a suspect or interviewee on the handling or conduct of police interviews unless they have complied with trainings of the BSB.

If requested to perform such work when not qualified to do so you <u>must</u> refuse the instructions if there is not one suitably qualified to accompany you as you would otherwise be acting in breach of CD7.

The training for privately funded police station work is the Police Station Qualification and in addition the barrister must hold a Magistrates Court Qualification if they do not hold a higher right of audience. On the other hand for publicly funded police work they need to complete the trainings specified by the Legal Aid Agency.

## 2.6.2 Public Access Work

Similarly, you must not undertake Public Access Work without successfully completing the required training specified by the BSB. In order to undertake Public Access Work you:

a) <u>Must</u> hold a full practising certificate
b) If you are less than three years standing you <u>must</u> have a qualified person readily available to you to provide guidance if necessary;
c) <u>Must</u> notify the Bar Council of your intention to undertake such work; and
d) Have adequate insurance cover.

It is important to note that you would be in breach of CD 3 and 4 if you caused or permitted your client to believe that you are entitled to or will provide services that include the Public Access Work if you are not entitled to undertake such work.

You cannot accept public access instructions if you form the view that it is in the best interest of the client to instruct a solicitor.

## 2.6.3 Criminal advocacy

In order to undertake criminal advocacy you must be accredited to the correct Quality Assurance Scheme for Advocates (QASA) level.

# CHAPTER 3

## The Duty to the Court in the Administration of Justice (CD 1)

### 3.1  Overriding obligation to the Court

There is an overriding duty to the Court to act with independence and in the interest of justice that has primacy over any inconsistent obligation other than under criminal law. This applies irrespective of the role the BSB regulated person has in the conduct of litigation or advocacy before a Court.

This includes the following obligations:

a)  You must not knowingly or recklessly mislead or attempt to mislead the Court;
b)  You must not abuse your role as advocate;
c)  You must take reasonable steps to ensure that the Court has all relevant decisions and legislative provisions before it;
d)  You must ensure that your ability to act independently is not compromised.

When considering how to best serve the interest of the client a barrister needs to consider his/her competing obligations notwithstanding the views of your client, professional client, employer or any other person. It is important to note that all barristers are personally responsible for their own conduct and professional work. You <u>must</u> use your own professional judgment in relation to those matters on which you are instructed and be able to justify your decisions and actions.

## 3.2 Conflict between the duty to the client and the duty to the Court

You are obliged by CD 2 to promote and protect the best interest of your client so far as it is consistent with the law and with the overriding duty to the Court under CD 1.

As such you can put forward your client's case even if you do not believe the facts as your client states them as long as the positive case you put forward accords with your instructions and you do not knowingly or reckless mislead the Court.

### 3.2.1 Duty not to knowingly or recklessly mislead the Court

You must not:

a) make submissions, representations or statements;
b) ask questions which suggest facts to witnesses which you know are untrue or misleading; or
c) call witnesses, put affidavits or statements to the Court which you know or are instructed are untrue or misleading.

The duty not to knowingly or recklessly mislead the Court is mandatory and includes a duty not to permit the Court to be misled.

Knowingly misleading the Court means that you cannot intentionally or inadvertently mislead the Court. Furthermore, if you realise that you have mislead the Court you have an obligation to correct the position as it will otherwise amount to knowingly misleading the Court in breach of the Handbook.

Recklessly misleading the Court is also not allowed. This includes being indifferent to the truth.

This duty applies for the whole duration of the case. If you discovered during a case that you had inadvertently misled the Court you must correct the position.

### 3.2.1.1 Conflicting witness evidence

If a witness gives conflicting statement to evidence previously given, you can draw the witness' attention to the conflicting evidence and say the Court may find it difficult to accept. But if the evidence is true, you can ask the witness to confirm the statement and will not be misleading the Court.

In the situation where you client changes his/her version of the facts, you may continue to act unless it is clear to you that your client is attempting to put forward false evidence. Whether or not you believe the client is irrelevant but you must be careful not to mislead the Court and if you know that the conflicting statement is false evidence you cannot put it before the Court.

### 3.2.1.2 Hostile witness

If a witness turns hostile you can point this to the Court and will not be misleading.

## 3.2.2 Duty to take reasonable steps to ensure that the Court has all relevant decisions and legislative provisions before it

You must take reasonable steps to ensure that the Court has all relevant decisions and legislative provisions before it.

If you become aware, at any point during the case of any decision or provision which <u>may</u> be adverse to the interest of your client, you <u>must</u> draw the Court's attention to it. This is particularly important in the case where you are appearing against a litigant not legally represented. In such a case, your duty to the Court overrides your duty to act in the best interest of your client. You must also avoid wasting the time of the Court by bringing it to its attention as soon as practicable.

If a barrister becomes aware of the existence of a document which should have been disclosed but has not been disclosed, on discovery of the document s/he should advise his/her professional client to disclose it forthwith; and if it is not then disclosed, s/he must withdraw from the case.

It must be noted that this obligation extends to your opponent's case to the extent that it concerns legislative provisions and relevant decisions. However, you have no obligation to remedy the failure of your opponent to put his/her case on the evidence in a competent matter and doing so would amount to a breach of CD2 and CD7 on your part since you have an obligation to act in the best interest of your own client.

### 3.2.3  Discovery of a new authority which undermines the case

If in the course of a case you discover new authority undermines your case and your opponent or the Judge is unaware of it you <u>must</u> disclose it to your opponent and to the Court, even if this means your client will lose the case. Failure to do so and to continue with your submissions would be to mislead the Court.

### 3.2.4  Disqualified juror

If you discover that one of the jurors is disqualified from service under the Juries Act 1974 or biased, your duty to the Court requires you to inform the Court thereof <u>at the earliest opportunity</u>. Please note that a previous conviction of juror is a matter of public record and would be information which you can disclose to the Court irrespective of any legal privilege you may have had with the juror in question.

## 3.2.5 Duty not abuse your role as advocate

Although you must put forward your client's case to the best of your abilities you must not abuse your role as an advocate.

As such, you must not put forward a personal opinion of the facts or the law unless invited or required to do so by the Court or by law.

### 3.2.5.1 Arguments without merit

You should not pursue legal arguments that you do not consider have any merit and that you do not consider is properly arguable or supported even if your client insists that you do so.

### 3.2.5.2 Insulting, humiliating or annoying witnesses

You cannot make statements or ask questions <u>merely to insult, humiliate or annoy</u> a witness or other person. You should also note that you cannot give your personal opinion on the facts at any point.

Similarly, you cannot put any question or assertion you like to a witness even if you feel it might assist your case because this would amount to abusing your role as advocate. This is a cross cutting principle that is relevant to other modules of the BPTC such as advocacy.

If your client requests that you put some questions which you do not think are appropriate or relevant, you should explain to him/her that here are certain limitation to your duty to act in his/her best interest and you <u>must</u> refuse to do so in order not to abuse your role as an advocate. If the client insists, this would amount to the client attempting to limit your independence in conducting the proceedings and/or requiring you to act in contravention to the provisions of the Handbook which would require you to cease to act and return your instructions.

### 3.2.5.3 *Making serious allegations against any person*

You <u>must not</u> make <u>serious</u> allegations against a witness you had a chance to cross examine unless you gave him/her a chance to answer the allegations in cross-examinations.

In relation to specific allegations against a person or suggestions that the person is guilty of an offence of which your client is charged, you must not make such an allegation unless:

    a)   There are <u>reasonable</u> grounds for the allegation;
    b)   It is relevant to your client's case;
    c)   It is relevant to the credibility of a witness.

If the allegations concerns a third party to the proceedings you should avoid naming them in open Court unless it is <u>reasonably necessary.</u>

## 3.3 Conflict between the duty of confidentiality and the duty to the Court

The duty to the Court does not authorise you to disclose information which you have obtained in the course of your instructions and which your client has not authorised you to disclose to the Court (which is therefore subject to Legal Professional Privilege). As part of your duty to your client (CD2) you also have a duty to protect the confidentiality of each client's affairs, except for such disclosures as are required or permitted by law or to which your client gives informed consent.

Your duty of confidentiality continues after the Counsel-client relationship has ended. Clients who put their confidence in their legal advisers must be able to do so in the knowledge that the information they give, or which is given on their behalf, will stay confidential.

As such, when considering the proper course of action you must weight your various obligations.

### 3.3.1 Admission of guilt in confidence

You cannot disclose information provided in confidence by the client, such as an admission of guilt to the Court without the client's consent.

However, you also cannot mislead the Court if a client who admitted guilt in confidence pleaded not guilty. You would still be allowed to:

a) test the reliability of prosecution evidence by cross examining the prosecution witness both on credibility and on the facts and

b) address the jury about the fact that prosecution did not prove the case to the required standard.

But you must not make a positive case inconsistent with the confession made in confidence. As such you cannot:

a) suggest to a prosecution witness that your client did not commit the crime or someone else did it;

b) call evidence showing that the client is innocent or someone else did it such as in a defence of mistaken identity;

c) submit to the jury that the client is innocent or someone else did it;

d) put forward an alibi.

If your client informs you that he/she wishes to plead guilty despite the fact that he/she is innocent, you should attempt to dissuade him but if he/she insists, you can continue to represent him but there are restrictions on what you can say in the sentencing hearing in terms of mitigation. You cannot for example say that his/her guilty plea is evidence of remorse as the client has maintained his/her innocence to you. You <u>must not</u> inform the Court of the fact that he/she is in fact innocent, the motives of his/her guilty plea or that he/she has done so against your advice. This does not amount to misleading the Court.

Please note however that there is nothing in the Handbook which requires you to accede to a Judge's request that you breach confidentiality in the circumstances described.

### 3.3.2 Documents disclosed in confidence which could mislead the Court

If there is a risk the Court can be misled by documents obtained in confidence or of which you become aware, you should ask the client for permission to disclose it to the Court and inform him that if he/she refuses you <u>must</u> cease to act.

If client refuses you <u>must</u> cease to act, return your instructions and not reveal the document to the Court as you have a duty to keep the affairs of each client confidential.

You should explain the reasons for your withdrawal to the client.

### 3.3.3 Other information which could mislead the Court

In the situation where you learn of information relevant to the case which could mislead the Court and which you learned about in circumstances other than through privileged conversation, such as knowledge of violent character, you cannot mislead the Court. You must withdraw from the case on the basis of professional embarrassment.

If the information relates to criminal conduct you may wish to report the matter to the police as it may otherwise breach your duty to act in a way which is likely to diminish the trust and confidence which the public places in your and the profession although there is no obligation per se to report.

When applying these principles, the arguments can be both in favour of reporting or against reporting to the police.

### 3.3.4 Previous convictions disclosed in confidence

If the prosecution is not aware of a previous conviction of your client or breach of bail, which was disclosed to you in confidence, you should ask him for permission to disclose it to the Court.

Regardless of the nature of the case or potential sentence, Counsel should give the Defendant clear advice as to all the options.

He/she should:

a) Inform the Defendant that the information as to the previous conviction will remain confidential unless the client specifically waives privilege;

b) Inform the Defendant that whilst the information remains confidential, he/she will be restricted in what he/she can say in mitigation;

c) Advise the Defendant that nothing can be said as to the Defendant's record which expressly or impliedly adopts the position as outlined by the Prosecution and in particular, that nothing can be said as to:

- the absence of conviction of the type or gravity of the undisclosed conviction;

- a period of time as being free from convictions if the undisclosed conviction occurred during that period; and

- the absence of a particular sentence or disposal in the Defendant's antecedents if such sentence or disposal was in fact imposed in respect of the undisclosed conviction.

d) Specifically advise the Defendant as to the nature of the sentencing exercise if the Court became aware of the undisclosed conviction, whether by virtue of the Defendant's voluntary disclosure or by some other means;

e) Advise that if you are asked a direct question you must not give an untruthful answer and you will have to withdraw;

f) Advise the Defendant as to the possibility of the Prosecution subsequently discovering the undisclosed conviction;

g) Advise of the real possibility that failure of Counsel to refer to the Defendant's antecedents would not go unnoticed by experienced Prosecution Counsel or Judge.

This could lead to an adjournment, or to the matter being relisted for alteration of the sentence. The Defendant should be told that the choice as to what course to adopt is his, but that if he/she decides to reveal the qualifying conviction, he/she would be entitled to expect significant credit from the Court in fixing the sentence.

Note that if the client has not informed you of it but you have uncovered this on your own, the same Rules apply. There is no duty on you to divulge the previous conviction, although you must not mislead the Court in the process.

### 3.3.5 Previous convictions in cases of mandatory sentence

There is however an exception if there is a mandatory sentence which applies in the case and the failure to disclose will result in the Court failing to pass the sentence that is required by law. In this case you must ask for consent to disclose and advise your client that if he/she refuses you must cease to act.

## 3.4 Exceptions to the duty of confidentiality

You must preserve the confidentiality of the client's affairs "as permitted by law".

Your duty to confidentiality is subject to an exception if disclosure is required or permitted:

a) by law for instance pursuant to the Proceeds of Crime Act 2002. In such a case it would not amount to a breach of CD6; or
b) by the regulator.

If for instance your client informs you that he/she will commit an act of violence against a witness or a third party you must inform the police <u>if you are satisfied that the threat is genuine.</u>

It must be noted that if you are a pupil, the obligation of confidentiality is applied to you as if the client was your own client.

# CHAPTER 4

## THE DUTY TO ACT IN THE BEST INTERESTS OF EACH CLIENT, TO KEEP THE AFFAIRS OF EACH CLIENT CONFIDENTIAL AND PROVIDE A COMPETENT STANDARD OF WORK (CD 2, 6 AND 7)

Your duty to act in the best interests of each client (CD2) is subject to your duty to the Court (CD1) and to your obligations to act with honesty, and integrity (CD3) and to maintain your independence (CD4) and duty not to discriminate unlawfully against any person (CD8).

Therefore, when considering the interests of your client you must think of your other competing duties.

### 4.1 Duty to promote fearlessly and by all proper and lawful means the client's best interests

You <u>must</u> promote <u>fearlessly and by all proper and lawful means</u> the client's best interests <u>without regard to your own interests or to any consequences to you or to any other person</u>. It is important to note that your duty is to your client and not your professional client or other intermediary.

This duty extends to each and every client individually because you may only accept instructions to act for more than one client if you are able to act in the best interests of <u>each</u> client.

### 4.1.1 Duty to consider whether the client is best served by different legal representation

Your duty to act in the best interests of <u>each</u> client includes a duty to consider whether the client's best interests are served by different legal representation. Where this is the case, you <u>must</u> advise the client to that effect.

There are several reasons why your client's interest may be served by alternative representation including:

a) If your client needs a legal representative more senior or junior than you or with different expertise;
b) Your client needs more than one legal representative, or less than the number initially appointed.

If you are acting through a professional client, this duty includes advising your client to retain different solicitors if it is in his/her best interest. This advising your client that in their best interests they should be represented an advocate or legal representative, more senior or more junior than you, or with different experience from yours.

In case you are acting on a public access scheme you <u>must </u>also consider whether it is in your client's interest to instruct solicitors.

If you consider that your professional client, another solicitor or intermediary, another barrister, or any other person acting on behalf of your client has been negligent, you should ensure that your client is advised of this. Your duty is simply to advise your lay client, not the SRA or the Court.

### 4.1.2 Honest mistake by the opposing side

In case of an honest mistake by an opponent which benefits your client outside Court and which does not involve misleading the Court or the opponents, Counsel must promote and protect fearlessly the lay client's interests. Such an example includes where a an opposing Counsel advises you that his/her client is prepared to make an offer to settle for the sum bigger than what you initially expected the case to be worth as it is clear that your opponent has misunderstood a critical document/s and there is nothing on these facts to suggest that you are misleading your opponent. You should therefore settle the case for the bigger sum proposed without raising the issue with the opposing Counsel as you must promote fearlessly and by all proper and lawful means the client's best interests.

## 4.2 Duty not to permit your professional client, employer or any other person to limit your discretion as to how the interests of the client can best be served

You are personally responsible for your own conduct and for your professional work. You must not permit your professional client, employer or any other person to limit your discretion as to how the interests of the client can best be served.

You must use your professional judgment to meet your obligations at all times in relation to the matters on which you are instructed and be able to justify your decisions and actions. You must do this notwithstanding the views of your client, professional client, employer or any other person.

It is important to note that this includes the client. If the client for instance is of the opinion that a witness should be called, and in your professional judgement this would undermine the case, due for instance to the previous convictions of the witness, you must use your professional judgement and carry you case irrespective of the views of your client.

Even in cases where you are instructed by a professional client, your duty to the lay client supersedes your duty to the professional client.

This combined with your duty to act in the best interest of the client means that in some case you need to act against the course of action recommended by the professional client if it is not in the client's best interest.

A barrister acting for a Defendant should advise his/her client as to whether or not to give evidence in his/her own defence but the decision must be taken by the client themselves. An inference may be drawn against him/her if s/he does not.

## 4.3  Duty to provide a competent standard of work

In addition to the obligations mentioned above to act in the best interest of each client, providing a competent standard of work involves several considerations.

### 4.3.1  Closing Speech

This includes ensuring that the closing speech includes all the allegations supporting your case and that you do not present a closing speech without hearing the prosecution closing and the Judge's summing up. This would otherwise breach both your duty under CD 7 and your duty to act in the best interest of the client as well as your duty to assist the Court in the administration of justice.

Counsel prosecuting an unrepresented Defendant should draw the Court's attention to any mitigation they may be aware of but should not, unless asked, express a personal view of the merits of the case.

### 4.3.2  Continuing Professional Development requirements

In order to provide a competent standard of work you should keep your professional knowledge and skills up to date and regularly take part in professional development and educational activities that maintain and further develop competence and performance.

Any Practising Barrister who starts practice on or after the 1st October 2001 must during the first three years in which he/she holds a practising certificate after any pupillage, complete a <u>minimum of 45 hours</u> of CPD.

Thereafter if he/she holds a practising certificate he/she must complete <u>a minimum of 12 hours</u> of CPD per calendar year. If he/she only holds a practicing certificate for part of the year he/she must complete <u>one hour</u> of CPD <u>for each month</u> for which he/she holds a certificate.

However, merely complying with the Continuing Professional Development requirements may not be sufficient to comply with your obligations to provide a competent standard of work. You may for instance be fully up-to-date with your CPD requirements but fail to provide a competent standard of work by failing to be aware of relevant authorities. In such a case you would be liable to disciplinary action if a complaint is brought forward.

You must note however that there is no requirement for additional specialist training.

### 4.3.3 Outsourcing and delegation

Your obligations under the Handbook still allow you to delegate or outsource discrete tasks to other individuals where appropriate however, you remain responsible for any work delegated or outsourced.

You remain responsible for any work delegated or outsourced and are responsible for the services provided by all those who represent you in your dealings with your clients or any other employees, pupils or agents. You cannot blame pupils for mistakes they have made or blame the tight time schedules as you should have returned the instructions if the work could not be done in the stipulated time.

Where you outsource to a third party any support services critical to the delivery of any legal services it does not alter your obligation to the client and you remain responsible for compliance with the Handbook.

You <u>must</u> ensure that it is subject to contractual agreements which:

a) Protect the confidentiality of the client in accordance with your own obligations;
b) Complies with any other obligations which may be relevant;
c) Processes any personal data in accordance with instruction and in line with the Data Protection Act as though it were a data controller.

There is also an obligation to allow the BSB or its agent to obtain information from, inspect records and enter the premises of such third party in relation to the activities outsourced.

It must however be noted that this does not apply where the client has a separate agreement with the third party for the outsourcing.

### 4.3.4  Competent standard of service

Your duty to provide a competent standard of work includes a duty to provide competent service to your client. You should remember that your client may not be familiar with legal proceedings. You should do what you <u>reasonably</u> can to ensure that your client understands the process and what to expect from your service and the process of providing such service in order to avoid <u>any unnecessary distress</u>. This is particularly important when dealing with a <u>vulnerable</u> client.

Providing a competent standard of service includes:

a) Treating client with courtesy and consideration;
b) Seeking to advise your clients in terms they understand;
c) Taking all reasonable steps to avoid unnecessary expenses;
d) Reading your instructions promptly and properly.

### 4.3.5  Reading instructions promptly

You <u>must</u> read your instructions promptly as you may otherwise not be aware of time limits applicable in the relevant case.

Your duty to provide a competent standard of work and service in this case includes a duty to inform your professional client or lay client <u>as far as reasonably possible</u> in sufficient time to enable appropriate steps to be taken to protect the client's interests if:

a) it <u>becomes apparent</u> that you will not be able to carry out the instructions <u>within the time requested or within a reasonable time after receipt of the instructions</u>; or

b) there is an <u>appreciable risk</u> that you <u>may</u> not be able to undertake the instructions.

### 4.3.6  Clash of hearing dates listing

Your duty to provide a competent standard of work and service to each client (CD7) includes a duty to inform your professional client, or your lay client if instructed directly, <u>as soon as reasonably possible</u> to enable appropriate steps to be taken to protect the client's interests, if:

a) it becomes apparent to you that you will not be able to carry out the instructions within the time requested, or within a reasonable time after receipt of instructions; or

b) there is an <u>appreciable risk</u> that you may not be able to undertake the instructions.

If you are a self-employed barrister and despite all reasonable efforts to prevent it, a hearing becomes fixed for a date on which you have already entered in your professional diary that you will not be available, you <u>may</u> cease to act and return your instructions. This may include a prior arranged hearing relating to another case.

You should try to make <u>all reasonable efforts</u> to prevent a clash of dates. This involves communicating effectively with the Court and managing and diarising your cases effectively.

Where it is impossible to prevent a clash of hearing dates, you <u>must</u> exercise your professional judgement in deciding which hearing is most important to attend.

Particular types of hearings may have to take precedence as a matter of law or procedure. You <u>should</u> take direction from the Court and have regard to any relevant case management rules.

Where an order of precedence is not clear, you <u>should</u> consider:

    a)   your duty to act in the best interests of each of your clients and,
    b)   which of you clients is likely to be <u>most prejudiced</u> by alternative representation being arranged <u>at short notice</u>.

In addition to the following factors relating to each case should be considered:

- the length of time that you have been instructed on each case;
- the complexity and difficulty of each case;
- the amount of work you have already done on the case; and
- relevant <u>access to justice</u> considerations and the likely impact on your client.

Special consideration should also be given to the needs of <u>vulnerable clients</u>.

Where you are unable to attend a hearing date, you should take all reasonable steps to assist clients to find alternative representation.

It is to be noted that where a hearing lasts longer than anticipated, and the only other commitment in your professional diary are your holidays, you should not request a postponement as that would amount to wasting the time of the Court. You should instead cancel your holidays to attend the hearing.

In long trials, where after the conclusion of the opening speech by the Prosecution, defending Counsel is satisfied that during a specific part of the trial there is no serious possibility that events will occur which will relate to his/her client, he/she may with the consent of the professional client (or his/her representative) and of the lay client absent himself for that part of the trial. He/she should also inform the Judge but is not required to seek the Judge's permission.

In this event it is his/her duty:

a) to arrange for other defending Counsel to guard the interests of his/her client;
b) to keep himself informed throughout of the progress of the trial and in particular of any development which could affect his/her client; and
c) not to accept any other commitment which would render it impracticable for him to make himself available at reasonable notice if the interests of his/her client so require.

### 4.3.7 Arriving late to Court

Arriving on time to Court involves both the duty not to waste the Court's time and the duty to provide a competent standard of work. If you know you are about to be late to a Court hearing you should:

a) call you client and/or instructing solicitor to notify them that you would be late pursuant to CD 2 and CD7;

b) contact the Court to inform them pursuant to CD 1.

In order to protect the client's best interests you should request that the Court proceedings do not start until you have arrived. It must also be noted that providing a competent standard of service includes treating your client with courtesy and consideration.

### 4.3.8 Confidentiality Guidance

All client communications are privileged and that such communications, client information and Chambers confidential data (financial or otherwise) must be stored, handled and disposed of securely.

The Handbook requires barristers to preserve the confidentiality of the client's affairs. Any barrister who does not adhere to this by, for example, allowing other people to see confidential material, losing portable devices on which unprotected information is stored, or not disposing of client papers securely could face disciplinary action by the BSB.

Barristers are data controllers under the Data Protection Act and must comply with the requirements of the Act in handling data to which that Act applies. They are responsible for the conduct of those who undertake work on their behalf and are advised to ensure that clerks and other Chambers' staff are aware of the need to handle and dispose of confidential material securely.

Chambers <u>must</u> also have <u>appropriate</u> data management systems for looking after confidential information.

In making arrangements to look after the information entrusted to them, barristers should seek to <u>reduce the risk of casual or deliberate unauthorised access</u> to it. Consideration needs to be given to information kept in electronic form as well as on paper.

The arrangements should cover:

- The handling and storage of confidential information.
- Suitable arrangements should be made for distributing papers and sending faxes and emails.
- Particular care should be taken when using removable devices such as laptops, removable discs, CDs, USB memory sticks and Personal Digital Assistant (PDAs).
- When no longer required, all confidential material must be disposed of securely, for example by returning it to the client or professional client, shredding paper, permanently erasing information no longer required and securely disposing of any electronic devices which hold confidential information.

Papers should not be left where others can read them, and computers should be placed so that they cannot be overlooked, <u>especially when working in public places</u>. When not being used, papers should be stored in a way which <u>minimises the risk of unauthorised access</u>. Computers should be password protected. There should be suitable arrangements in place for distributing papers and sending faxes and emails while protecting confidentiality.

Devices used to store information should be used to store <u>only information needed for immediate business purposes</u>, not for permanent storage. Information on them should be <u>at least password protected</u> and <u>preferably encrypted</u>. Great care should be taken in looking after the devices themselves to ensure that they are not lost or stolen.

Additional safeguards will need to be put in place for particularly sensitive information, or for cases in which Counsel from the same Chambers are appearing on opposing sides.

### 4.3.9  No duty to members of Chambers

It is important to note that there is no 'Counsel to Counsel' confidentiality. As such any information you may learn from a fellow counsel that is relevant to your client should be shared with the client and used in his/her best interest. This situation is different from obtaining access to privileged confidential information.

# CHAPTER 5

## ACCEPTING AND RETURNING INSTRUCTIONS

In the light of your duty to act in the best interest of your client (CD2) the Handbook regulates the circumstances in which you can accept and return instructions.

A distinction must be made between situations where you are appointed by a lay client and working on a referral basis and the situation in which you are appointed by a professional client to provide legal services on behalf of one of the professional client's own client.

## 5.1 Situations where you must not accept instructions

You <u>must</u> distinguish between situation where you <u>must not</u> accept instructions, situations where you <u>must accept</u> instructions (Cab Rank Rule) and situations where you <u>may not</u> accept instructions.

You <u>must not</u> accept instructions if:

a) There is a conflict of interest with your own interest or the interests of a previous or existing client;
b) Due to an existing or previous instructions you are not able to fulfil your obligation to act in the best interest of the prospective client;

c) There is a risk that information confidential to a former or existing client may be relevant to a prospective client such that you could not act in the best interest of each client;

d) Your instructions seek to limit your ordinary authority or discretion in the conduct of proceedings in Court;

e) Your instructions require you to act other than in accordance with the law or the Handbook;

f) You are not authorised, accredited, competent or experienced enough to perform the work required;

g) You do not have enough time to deal with the particular matter;

h) There is a real prospect you are not going to be able to maintain your independence.

## 5.1.1 Conflict of interest with your own interests

You are prohibited from acting where there is a conflict of interest between the prospective client and your own personal interests.

### 5.1.1.1 Material commercial interest

This may happen for instance where you have a material commercial interest in an organisation which is proposing to refer a matter to you.

A material commercial interest is an interest which an objective observer with knowledge of the salient facts would reasonably consider might potentially influence your judgement. Any interest in an organisation such as being an owner or manger would fall under this definition.

In case you have a material interest in an organisation which proposes to refer a matter to you, you must:

a) Inform the client in writing about your interest in that organisation before you accept the instructions;

b) Make a clear agreement with the organisation about how relevant issues such as conflicts of interest will be deal with; and

a) Keep a record of your referrals to any such organisation for review by the BSB on request.

You may only refer a client to an organisation in which you have a material commercial interest if it is in the client's best interest as it would otherwise be in breach of CD2. In addition, CD3 requires you to be open with the client about any interest you have in or arrangements you have with the organisation.

Where you have <u>a material commercial interest</u> in an organisation to which you plan to refer a client you <u>must</u>:

a) Tell the client <u>in writing</u> about your interest in that organisation before you refer the client;

b) Keep a record of your referrals to any such organisation for review by the BSB on request ; and

c) Ensure that the client is not wrongly led to believe that the organisation is subject to the regulations of the BSB or another approved regulator if it is not the case.

It must be noted that a referral agreement obliging you to refer clients to an organisation, whether or not you have an interest in that organisation, would not be justifiable as being in the best interest of each client and as such would breach both your duty to your client under CD2 and your obligation of honesty and integrity under CD3 and compromise your independence under CD4.

### 5.1.1.2 Advice detrimental to the barrister

If a situation arises where after accepting instructions, advising your client of a particular course of action which is in his/her best interest would be detrimental to you, you <u>may</u> continue to act but <u>must</u> inform your client of your advice which would be in his/her best interest. Not informing him/her would amount to a breach of your obligation to act in the best interest of your client as you do not have the discretion as to whether to communicate this or not.

### 5.1.1.3 Member of chamber party to a case

In the situation where a member of your chambers is a party to the case, you must refuse instructions if you consider that your independence is compromised. However, you must also consider that the mere fact that you know a party to a case may not be enough to refuse instructions. You must note here that the Cab Rank Rule does not apply in situations where you must refuse to accept instructions.

## 5.1.2 Conflict of interest with existing or previous client

### 5.1.2.1 Confidentiality

Your duty to maintain confidentiality is owed to each of your clients. Your duty of confidentiality continues after the Counsel-client relationship has ended. Clients who put their confidence in their legal advisers must be able to do so in the knowledge that the information they give, or which is given on their behalf, will stay confidential.

You must not accept the instructions where there is a conflicting interest between an existing or previous client and a prospective one, whether in relation to your duties to the respective clients or in relation to confidentiality.

You must refuse to take the case if there is a real risk that information confidential to one client may be relevant to the prospective client.

You <u>may</u> be entitled to accept the intrusions or to continue to act on the matter if:

a) You have fully disclosed to both clients the extent and nature of the conflict;
b) Both have provided their informed consent to you acting despite the conflict of interest;
c) You are able to act in the best interest of each client; and
d) You are able to act independently.

### 5.1.2.2 Representing clients who disagree

Where you are representing two clients and one of them is of a different opinion on a matter relating to a case such as settlement, you cannot continue to act for both clients because a clear conflict of interests has arisen. You can potentially continue to act for clients who are in conflict where they give their informed consent for you to continue acting. However, if you are unable to act in the best interests of each client as if they were your only client you must withdraw and clearly explain to your client or professional client your reasons for doing so.

### 5.1.2.3 Joint Defendants in criminal cases

If you are instructed to represent two Defendants in a criminal trial where one Defendant asserts self-defence and the other claims the defence of alibi and names his/her co-Defendant as his/her alibi witness there is an obvious conflict of interest. The same applies where one client blames the other which you are also representing. In such cases, you should withdraw because of the conflict of interest between your clients.

### 5.1.2.4 *Other cases which do not amount to a conflict of interest*

Being instructed to represent two defendants where one has a representation order and the other is a private payer does not constitute a conflict of interest.

## 5.1.3 Not authorised, accredited, competent or experienced

If you are not qualified or sufficiently experienced to accept instructions in relation to a matter, you must not accept the instructions. Examples are Public Access Work, criminal advocacy or police station attendance. If requested to perform such work when not qualified to do so you must refuse the instructions if there is not one suitably qualified to accompany you as you would otherwise be acting in breach of CD7 if you were to attend alone.

Another situation may be where the instructions would require you to conduct correspondence with parties other than your client which you do not have adequate systems, experience or resources to manage appropriately.

Your competency to work with clients includes your ability to work with vulnerable clients which may require special attention.

It must be noted that it is the barrister's judgment that matters in relation to whether he/she is competent or not and not the solicitor's.

In situations where the instructions relate to an area in which you have no experience, such as a civil case after you have completely an exclusively criminal pupillage, you are not competent to undertake the work required and must not accept the instructions. Doing otherwise would amount to a breach of CD2, CD5 and CD7.

Please note that you are not entitled to refuse to accept instructions merely because you usually act on behalf of one particular party such as the police.

## 5.1.4 Late instructions

Your duty to provide a competent standard of work and service to each client (CD7) includes a duty to inform your professional client, or your lay client if instructed directly, <u>as soon as reasonably possible </u>to enable appropriate steps to be taken to protect the client's interests, if:

a) it becomes apparent to you that you will not be able to carry out the instructions within the time requested, or within a reasonable time after receipt of instructions; or

b) there is an <u>appreciable risk</u> that you may not be able to undertake the instructions.

Therefore, if at the time of receiving the instruction you are aware that there is an <u>appreciable risk</u> that you may not be able to undertake the instructions you <u>must not </u>take the instructions. This includes if you already have holidays in your professional calendar and will not have time to perform to the best interest of the client.

If under exceptional circumstances when instructions are delivered <u>so late that no suitable, competent advocate would have adequate time to prepare</u>, you are not required to refuse instructions as it will be in the best interest of the client that you accept. If you are obliged by the Cab Rank Rule to accept you must do so.

## 5.1.5 Compromised independence

If you may not be able to maintain your independence in putting forward the best interests of your client you <u>must not</u> take the case.

### 5.1.5.1 Risk of being called as a witness

This may arise if for instance you are likely to be called as a witness in the case.

If however the matter on which you are likely to be called as a witness is peripheral or minor in the context of the litigation as a whole and is unlikely to lead to your involvement in the matter being challenged at a later date, you may still act for your client.

You must also bear in mind, if you are planning to withdraw because you are likely to be a witness on a material question of fact that you <u>should</u> only withdraw <u>without jeopardizing the client's interest.</u>

It is important to note that you <u>must</u> promote <u>fearlessly and by all proper and lawful means</u> the client's best interests <u>without regard to your own interests or to any consequences to you or to any other person</u>. Your duty is to your client and not your professional client or other intermediary.

If you attend a client in a police station you may only accept the instructions, as long as you reasonably believe that nothing was said, done, heard or seen by you at the police station which might require you to give evidence in the proceedings.

### 5.1.5.2 Negligent professional client

If you are acting through a professional client, this duty includes advising your client to retain different solicitors if it is in his/her best interest, such as where the professional client is acting negligently.

If you consider that your professional client, another solicitor or intermediary, another barrister, or any other person acting on behalf of your client has been negligent, you should ensure that your client is advised of this. Your duty is simply to advise your lay client, not the SRA or the Court. You should also notify your instructing solicitor that you will be doing so.

This includes advising the client about potential disciplinary action against the professional client if any and in relation to damages.

### 5.1.5.3 Threats against the barrister

If your client threatens you, you should explain to him/her that this is unethical. You should stay calm and polite and should avoid allowing the atmosphere to escalate, and if you consider the threat to be genuine you must return your instructions if they affect your independence.

## 5.2 Cab Rank Rule

The Cab Rank Rule is the obligation on barristers to accept instructions from a client regardless of any personal dislike of the client or the case, etc. and is an analogy for the principle that a cab (taxi) available for hire cannot refuse to carry a passenger unless there are particular circumstances.

However, the analogy only applies to barristers, as a client through his/her solicitor, is at liberty to instruct whomever he wishes.

The Cab Rank Rule is to prevent any unjustified restrictions on the client's choice of barrister to protect the interests of clients, not the interests of barristers.

The Cab Rank Rule concerns only whether and when barristers are obliged to accept instructions. It does not concern the different situation, as to whether and when barristers once they have accepted instructions may become entitled or obliged to return instructions or withdraw from a case.

If none of the circumstances discussed above whereby you are obliged to refuse instructions apply, the Cab Rank Rule states that you <u>must</u> accept those instructions if:

a) You receive instructions from a professional client; <u>and</u>
b) You are self-employed or BSB authorised; <u>and</u>
c) The instructions are appropriate taking into account your experience, seniority and/or field or practice.

You <u>must</u> accept irrespective of:

a) The identity of the client;
b) The nature of the case to which the instructions relate;
c) Whether the client is paying privately or is publicly funded; and
d) Any belief or opinion which you may have formed as to the <u>character, reputation, cause, conduct, guilt or innocence</u> of the client.

It is important to note that breaching the Cab Rank Rule also amounts to a violation of your duty not to discriminate pursuant to CD8.

You <u>must not</u> withhold your services or permit your services to be withheld:

a) On the grounds that the nature of the case is objectionable to you <u>or to any section of the public</u>;
b) On the ground that the conduct, opinions or beliefs of the prospective clients are unacceptable to you <u>or to any section of the public</u>;
c) On <u>any</u> ground relating to the source of <u>any</u> financial support which may properly be given to the prospective client for the proceedings in questions.

Notwithstanding your preference for cases, if the instructions are appropriate to your experience, seniority and field of practice you <u>must</u> therefore accept them.

You are only obliged to accept instructions where you are being asked to act on <u>either</u> the Standard Contractual Terms <u>or</u> if you publish standard terms of work, on those terms.

The Cab Rank Rule also applies to instructions from any professional client as <u>all</u> authorised persons must be able to access this Rule on behalf of their clients in the same way, even if the authorised person is not regulated by the SRA. In that case the references to the SRA or its Code are references to that person's approved regulator and its regulatory arrangements.

There are however exceptions to the Cab Rank Rule where you may refuse to accept instructions without being in breach of your duties.

## 5.3 Situations where you may refuse to accept instructions

You <u>may</u> refuse to accept instructions if:

a) The instructions would require you to do something <u>other than in the course of your ordinary work</u> (such as foreign work, acting for a foreign lawyer –other than from the EU, Scotland or Northern Ireland, working on weekends) or to cancel a commitment already in your <u>professional diary;</u>

b) The potential liability for professional negligence exceeds the level of the professional indemnity cover which is reasonably available and likely to be available in the market for you to accept;

c) You have not been offered a proper fee for your services;

d) You are a QC and your instructions would require you to act without a junior in circumstances where it is in the best interest of a client to have a junior also instructed;

e) The professional client does not accept liability for your fees;

f) The professional client represents <u>in your reasonable opinion</u> an <u>unacceptable credit risk;</u>

g) The professional client is instructing you in their capacity as lay client.

The Cab Rank Rule does not apply where you are to be paid directly by the Legal aid Agency or the Crown Prosecution Service and:

a) Your fees have not been agreed;

b) You required to have your fees paid before you accept the instructions and the fees were not paid;

c) Accepting the instructions would require you to act other than in the Standard Contractual Terms or the terms published on your website.

### 5.3.1 Proper fees

The appropriateness of fees shall be considered having regard to:

a) The complexity, length and difficulty of the case;
b) Your ability experience and seniority; and
c) The expenses which you will incur.

It is important to note that you may refuse to accept instructions on the basis that you will not work under a conditional fee agreement or damages based agreement.

Whilst you may refuse to accept instructions on the basis that the fee is not a proper one, if the instructions are on the basis that you will do the work under a conditional fee agreement or damages based agreement, this does not permit refusal of a conditional fee brief in circumstances that amount to discrimination.

However, whether the case is publicly or privately funded is irrelevant as long as the fee is proper. The Cab Rank Rule applies whether the client is paying privately or is publicly funded. It is important to note that breaching this Rule also amounts to a violation of your duty not to discriminate pursuant to CD8.

You must make or accept any fee proposal within a reasonable time after receiving the instructions. If you do not do so you can no longer refuse to accept instructions on the ground that it does not amount to proper fees.

## 5.3.2 Credit risk of professional client

A professional client may represent an <u>unacceptable credit risk</u> if:

a) They are included on the Bar Council's list of Defaulting Solicitors;

b) <u>To your knowledge a barrister</u> has obtained a judgment against a professional client which remains unpaid<u>;</u>

c) There is evidence of other unsatisfied judgements that<u> reasonably call into question the professional client's ability to pay your fees;</u>

d) The professional client is subject to<u> insolvency proceedings, an involuntary arrangement or partnership voluntary agreement.</u>

Even where the above indications exist you should not arrive to a conclusion without considering alternative methods of mitigating the risks, such as seeking advance payment or payment into an escrow account.

## 5.3.3 Professional indemnity limit

The Guidance on Insurance and Limitation of Liability provides that barristers may limit or exclude their liability<u> in ways that are permitted at law</u>. However, they must be careful in relation to the implications of their exclusions of limitations of liability in relation to the Consumer Rights Act 2015. If a barrister is found by the Court to have limited liability in a way which is in breach of the Consumer Rights Act 2015, it may amount to professional misconduct.

Barristers in independent practice should regularly review the amount of their professional indemnity insurance cover, taking into account the type of work which they undertake and the likely liability for negligence. They should be aware that claims can arise many years after the work was undertaken and that they would be prudent to maintain adequate insurance cover for that time since cover operates on a "claims made" basis, and as such it is the policy and the limits in force at the time a claim is made that are relevant, not the policy and limits in force when the work was undertaken. They should also bear in mind the need to arrange run-off cover if they cease practice.

The Cab Rank Rule provides an exemption if the potential liability for professional <u>negligence</u> in respect of a particular matter could exceed the level of professional indemnity which is <u>reasonably available </u>and <u>likely to be available in the market for you to accept.</u>

It must be noted that you cannot accept the instructions and then subsequently increase or decrease the cover.

## 5.4 Steps when you accept instructions

Where you first accept instructions to act in a matter you <u>must</u> confirm <u>in writing</u>:

a) Acceptance of the instructions;
b) The terms on which you will be acting;
c) Basis of charging;
d) Their right to make a complaint, including to complain to the Legal Ombudsman (if it is the case) and the procedure to do so including time limits.

If the work is referral work you must also inform the client that he/she may complain directly to Chambers or the BSB authorised body without going through the solicitors.

The information requirement also applies when doing Public Access Work or to an intermediary if using one.

Where you are receiving instructions from a professional client you must send the required confirmation to the professional client and where you are instructed by a lay client to the latter. However, when doing referral work you do not need to give the professional client the information in a separate specific letter. It is enough to provide this information in the ordinary terms of reference letter which you send when you accept instructions. As for the lay client, if you do not send a letter of engagement, a specific letter must be sent giving the information above.

It is recommended that you summarise or refer to the scope of work you are instructed to undertake in your acceptance.

You must do so <u>before you begin work</u> unless it is <u>not reasonably practicable</u> in which case you should do so <u>as soon as reasonably practicable at the next appropriate opportunity.</u> This can be done by email.

If you are a self-employed barrister a clerk can confirm on your behalf your acceptance of the instructions.

## 5.4.1 The terms

You may refer the client or professional client to the terms of service set out on your website or to the Standard Terms of Service set out on the Bar Council Website.

The Bar Council Terms of Service have been written to delineate the responsibilities of the parties and to provide a comprehensive set of contractual terms. They are standard terms but barristers and SRA Authorised Persons are free to agree variations to them (or to agree entirely different terms) to suit their particular needs.

The new Standard Terms cannot be used:

a)  Where the lay client is to be party to the contract unless the lay client is the Authorised Person, or
b)  For publicly funded matters where the barrister is paid directly by the Legal Services Commission as part of the Community

Legal Service or as part of the Criminal Defence Service or by the Crown Prosecution Service.

Particular care must be exercised where barristers undertake work on terms that are different from the new Standard Terms to ensure that they do not assume duties or liabilities which are not covered by their professional indemnity insurance cover.

## 5.5 Amending instructions

Where the scope of the instructions is varied in accordance with the relevant client you are <u>not</u> required to confirm again in writing acceptance of the terms and basis on which you will be acting. You <u>will be deemed</u> to have accepted the instructions on the same terms or basis as before <u>when you begin work,</u> <u>unless otherwise specified.</u>

Where there is any variation in the instructions particular care should be taken to ensure that the client is clear about the basis for charging.

## 5.6 Returning instructions

Where you have accepted instruction to act, some situations may arise which may lead you to cease to act and others where you have an obligation to return the instructions.

### 5.6.1 Situations where you must return your instructions

You must return your instructions where:

a) A client refuses to authorise you to disclose some information to the Court which your duty to the Court requires you to do so;

b) You have become aware of the document which the client refuses to disclose and refuses to permit you to disclose. This is only applicable during the case.

c) You become aware that funding has been wrongly obtained by false or inaccurate information from Legal Aid and the client refuses to remedy the situation.

You will note that in cases where you become aware that funding was wrongly obtained, you should approach the client and inform him/her first that you must cease to act and return your instructions if he/she does not disclose or remedy the situation. This is applicable whether the case is a civil case or a criminal case. It must be noted that you cannot inform the Legal Aid services yourself after you cease to act.

Other scenarios where you must return your instructions are where your client requests that you put some questions which you do not think are appropriate or relevant you should explain to him/her that there are certain limitations to your duty to act in his/her best interest and you must refuse to do so in order not to abuse your role as an advocate. If the client insists, this would amount to the client attempting to limit your independence in conducting the proceedings and/or requiring you to act in contravention to the provisions of the Handbook which would require you to cease to act and return your instructions.

## 5.6.2 Situations where you may return your instructions

You may cease to act on a matter if:

a) Your professional conduct is being called into question

b) The client consents;

c) You do not receive payment when due;

d) There is some other substantial reason to do so;

e) You become aware of confidential or privileged information of another person which relates to the matter on which you are instructed;

f) You are a self-employed barrister <u>and despite all your reasonable efforts to prevent it</u> a hearing becomes fixed on a date which you have already entered in your professional diary;

g) You are a self-employed barrister <u>and</u> you experience <u>illness, injury, childbirth, a bereavement or similar matter</u> which makes you <u>unable reasonably</u> to perform the services required;

h) You are a self-employed barrister <u>and you are unavoidably required </u>to attend jury service.

It must be noted that as a self-employed barrister breaking an engagement to supply legal services for a reason other than the reasons mentioned above would amount to a breach of your duties.

### 5.6.2.1 *Professional conduct called into question*

You are entitled to withdraw from the case and return your instructions if your professional conduct has been called into question. If you do so you must clearly explain to your client or professional client your reasons for doing so.

Such an example includes where you client accuses you of incompetence without justification. You should speak to your client and find out why he/she has accused you of incompetence.

It is important to note that in such cases, you are also entitled to withdraw if the client/s consent.

### 5.6.2.2 *Client consent*

The client's consent is not required in all the cases before you return your instructions but is merely one of the circumstances which may lead you to return you instructions.

In case you are conducting litigation and you exercise your discretion to cease to act due to one of the circumstances above, your application to come off the record has to be approved by the Court.

However, if you are not conducting litigation, you can either obtain your client's consent or clearly explain to your client that you are returning your instructions.

Please note that in cases where you <u>must</u> return your instructions you are not required to obtain you client's consent.

### 5.6.2.3 Not receiving payment when due

If you did not receive payment when due in accordance with the terms or you gave reasonable notice requiring payment <u>and</u> made it clear to the client that failure to pay may result in you ceasing to act and returning your instructions, you may return your instructions.

It must be noted that if a fundamental change is made to your fees you should treat such a change as a withdrawal of your initial instructions and as though the client has replaced the instructions by new instructions on different terms.

Therefore, you must decide whether you are obliged to accept the instructions according to the Cab Rank Rule. If you are not obliged to accept the instructions you may decline the new instructions and you are not regarded as returning your instructions nor as having withdrawn on the matter because the previous instructions were withdrawn by the client.

However if you are obliged to accept the instructions, you must do so.

### 5.6.2.4 *Knowledge of confidential or privileged materials of the opposing side*

If you become aware of confidential and privileged information by accident, you should immediately return the document to the other side <u>without reading any further</u>.

According to *Ablitt v Mills and Reeve (A firm) and Another* ChD 24 Oct 1995, a solicitor receiving privileged documents where there had been an obvious mistake should return them.

In this case the solicitor who, on the client instructions reviewed the privileged information sent by error to him, was restrained from continuing to act as "it offends elementary notions of fairness and justice" if by knowingly taking advantage of the mistaken delivery of privileged papers a party to litigation although not itself told what those papers contain can continue to have the services of those who have read the papers and would be advising him.

According to the case of *English and American Insurance Co Ltd and Others v Herbert Smith* ChD1987 (1987) NLJ 148, <u>where privileged information had not yet been tendered in evidence</u> the <u>person entitled to legal professional privilege could restrain any use by the other side</u> including the use in pending proceedings.

In considering whether you can continue to act you must consider:

a)  Whether it is a case in which it is practical to apply for an injunction to prevent the use of the material as in *English and American Insurance*;

b)  Whether the use of the document was overt or covert, however since it would be impossible to forget information you have read, it might to some extent be used in the cross examination provided you are open with the Court and other side.

You should inform your client of the situation, explain to him/her that it would be unethical to keep the document as it would breach your duty to act with honesty and integrity and ask for his/her permission to disclose it to the Court, without revealing the information in the document preferably.

If the client refuses to allow you to disclose it to the Court you <u>must</u> cease to act and return your instructions as your client is trying to limit your independence and following his/her instructions would amount to knowingly misleading the Court in breach of CD1. In this case you cannot disclose to the Court that you have received the information.

Please note that if you come into possession of a document belonging to another party by some means other than the normal and proper channels, and have not read it, you should make enquiries of your professional client in order to ascertain the circumstances in which the document was obtained by the professional client. Unless satisfied that the document has been obtained in the ordinary course of events, you should immediately return the document unread to the person entitled to possession of it.

## 5.7 If the professional client who instructed you withdraws

It is important to note that where you have been appointed by a professional client and he/she withdraws you <u>cannot continue to act.</u> This counts as a situation where your instructions where withdrawn. You cannot act unless appointed by:

a) The Court;
b) Instructed by a new firms of solicitors; or
c) Directly instructed by the lay client on a public access basis.

You will not be bound by the Cab Rank Rule if appointed by the Court.

You should note that you can only be instructed on a Public Access Basis if you are qualified to carry out such instructions.

## 5.8  Steps when returning instructions

If you cease to act and return your instructions you should, <u>where possible and subject to your duty to the Court </u>ensure that the client is<u> not adversely affected </u>because there is not enough time to engage other <u>adequate </u>legal assistance.

You must not cease to act or return your instructions without either:

a)  Obtaining you client's consent or
b)  Clearly explaining to your client your reason for doing so.


## 5.9  Prohibition against returning instruction to anyone other than the client

It is important to note that you <u>must not</u> return your instructions to another person without the consent of either the lay client or the professional client who instructed you.

If you are in a situation where you intend to return the instruction you cannot pass them on to another barrister willing to take the case <u>without the consent of your client.</u>

# CHAPTER 6

## THE DUTY TO ACT WITH HONESTY AND INTEGRITY, TO MAINTAIN YOUR INDEPENDENCE AND NOT TO BEHAVE IN A WAY WHICH IS LIKELY TO DIMINISH THE TRUST AND CONFIDENCE WHICH THE PUBLIC PLACES IN YOU OR IN THE PROFESSION (CD 3, 4 AND 5)

Any conflicts between the duty to the client (CD2) and the duty to the Court (CD1) can only be resolved if you conduct yourself with honesty, integrity (CD3) and independence (CD4). You must not do anything which could reasonably be seen by the public to undermine your honesty, integrity (CD3) and independence (CD4).

You will remember in this respect that the duty to the client (CD2) is subject to your duty to maintain honesty, integrity (CD3) and independence (CD4).

There are a number of ways in which conduct would be <u>reasonably</u> perceived by the <u>public</u> as <u>undermining</u> honesty, integrity and independence. You will note that it is in this case the perception of the public which is relevant and as such this obligation is relevant to conduct outside the Courtroom in the course of professional life.

## 6.1 Duty not to knowingly or recklessly mislead or attempt to mislead anyone

You <u>must not</u> knowingly or recklessly mislead or attempt to mislead anyone. This obligation extends beyond the obligation not to mislead the Court. You must not:

a) Intentionally mislead;
b) Inadvertently mislead;
c) Negligently in a manner that is indifferent to the truth mislead and fail to correct the position when you realise it; or
d) Attempt to mislead anyone.

Deception by a BSB regulated person towards anyone amounts to a breach of CD 3 and 4 and possibly CD2 and CD5.

You must consider in this respect how matters will appear to the client.

If you become aware that you inadvertently misled the Court, you <u>must</u> inform it accordingly as well as your clients.

## Lack of clarity on the terms of service

If there is a lack of clarity as to whether the services are regulated, who is supplying them, on what terms and what redress the clients have and against whom, this may constitute a breach of CD2 and CD5. Clarifying the capacity in which you are providing the services and who is responsible for their provision is particularly important if you are a member of management as well as a barrister in your own right.

### 6.1.1 Charging incorrect rates

Similarly, if you were to charge rates applicable for barrister's hourly work for work done by a pupil, this would amount to a breach of CD3.

### 6.1.2 Sharing premises with other legal professionals or appearance of partnership

If self-employed barristers share offices with solicitors or other professionals without making <u>sufficiently</u> clear that they remain separate and independent from one another and are not responsible for one another's work, this may amount to a breach in CD 3,4 and possibly 5.

Similarly, a set of Chambers which fails to explain to unsophisticated lay clients that members of the Chambers are self –employed and responsible for their own work, creating the appearance of a partnership, this may amount to a breach of CD 3, 4 and possibly 5.

### 6.1.3 Inaccurate advertising

Knowingly or recklessly publishing advertising material which is inaccurate or likely to mislead could also result in breach of CD 3 and 4 and possibly 5.

## 6.2 Drafting legal documents and arguments

When drafting a statements of case, witness statements, affidavits or other documents a barrister must not:

a) Devise or plead facts other than those which you <u>reasonably</u> believe the witness would give if the witness were giving evidence <u>orally</u>;

b) Make allegations unsupported by your instructions and the evidence;

c) Plead fraud without clear instructions <u>and</u> sufficient evidence to raise a prima facie case; or

d) Make submissions that are not <u>properly</u> arguable.

If the solicitor includes statements which are inconsistent with your recollection of the events, you should not include them if they are not properly arguable on the evidence, not properly supported by the client or not likely to be given in oral evidence. Including the allegations without support would amount to a breach of your CD3.

It makes no difference if you are instructed to do so by your professional or lay client. You can only draft grounds if they are properly arguable and must take personal responsibility for your professional work.

Your client cannot compel you to draft grounds or arguments. This includes the right to refuse to draft appeal grounds where there are no such properly arguable points. In such cases, you should advise the client both orally of your view that there are no grounds of appeal and certify it in writing. The type of cases or source of funding are irrelevant in these particular circumstances.

If you are requested to draft a document under time constraint but have not received all the evidence, or are advised that more evidence will be communicated to you, or if you have been instructed that there is evidence in support, you can draft it but you should return the completed document marked "Draft" or with a letter or email making it clear this is a draft based upon the evidence which you have been told exists to support it. This however, does not apply to allegations of fraud for which you need credible material before you.

It is important to note that a barrister need not stick exactly to the wording of the proof of evidence, particularly where matters are poorly expressed there, provided the client has the chance to read through and confirm the draft before swearing it. Counsel has a duty to ensure that the content of the witness statement is not unnecessarily verbose or irrelevant, in accordance with the general duty to avoid wasting the Court's time.

## 6.3 Dealing with witnesses

### 6.3.1 Meeting witnesses

When calling a witness in support of your case you <u>must not</u> <u>rehearse, practice with or coach</u> a witness.

A barrister may speak to his/her own lay witnesses for the purpose of putting them at ease, if the barrister feels it is appropriate. It is permissible for witnesses to undergo witness familiarization – that is, given information about the Court process and shown around Court and told about the questioning process, in particular where the lay witness is a child or a vulnerable witness. This does not breach your CD1 or CD3.

You should avoid where possible discussing the evidence to be given or how to best give it. Although there is no longer any general Rule that a barrister should not discuss the case with a lay witness for his/her own case, it is generally to be avoided because of the inherent risks in doing so and may lead to suspicion of coaching. Whether or not you are accompanied by the legal representatives of the other side is irrelevant in this case.

It must be noted that experts are commonly spoken to in conference about their evidence without rehearsing, practicing with or coaching them.

### 6.3.2 Collecting evidence from witnesses

If a witness needs to be seen it may be best to meet them and discuss concerns they may have if you have already been supplied with a statement from your client in advance and in the presence of a representative from the professional client if there is one.

There is no longer a restriction on the ability of self-employed barristers to investigate and collect evidence generally and more specifically from taking statements from potential witnesses. You must take reasonable steps to avoid wasting the time of the Court and may do so even in the absence of the representatives of your solicitor's firm.

### 6.3.3  Bribing or influencing witnesses

You <u>must not</u> make or offer to make payments to witnesses which are contingent on the evidence the witness is giving.

You <u>must not</u> encourage a witness to give evidence which is <u>misleading or untruthful</u>.

### 6.3.4  Witnesses under oath

If the witness has been called to the stand and giving evidence you <u>must not</u>, during breaks, adjournments or Court recess, communicate about the case with any witness including your client if he/she:

a) Has not completed their evidence; <u>and</u>
b) Is still on oath, unless you have the permission of the representative for the <u>opposing side or of the Court. This includes your lay client.</u>

You should not ask your instructing solicitor to clarify the evidence with the witness under oath and pass the information on to you whilst the witness is giving evidence.

A barrister should not discuss the case with a lay witness for the other side, but can exchange pleasantries.

### 6.3.5 Impugning a witness

You must not challenge a witness unless you have put that point to the witness in cross examination or make <u>serious allegations</u> against any person unless such allegations are relevant to your case <u>and</u> are supported on <u>reasonable</u> grounds. This is so that the witness gets a chance to answer the allegation in cross examination. If this chance is not offered to a witness you cannot refer to it in your closing arguments, which you must do in order to act in the best interest of the client.

Serious allegations includes allegations of lying, or perverting evidence which could constitute an offence.

You should try where possible to call evidence to support the allegations but even where you do not do so you <u>must</u> put the matter to the witness in cross examination as you would otherwise act in breach of your duty to the Court in the administration of justice.

It must also be noted that even though you can make allegations in Court against a third party without mentioning them by name you cannot do so unless <u>reasonably necessary and </u>you have <u>reasonable grounds</u> for the allegation.

## 6.4 Corresponding with legal representatives

Where the opposing side is legally represented you are expected to correspond at all times with the other party's legal representative or you may be regarded as breaching your duty to act with honesty and integrity (CD3).

## 6.5 Making allegations of fraud

You <u>must not</u> make any allegation of fraud, unless you have <u>clear instructions</u> to allege fraud <u>and</u> you have <u>reasonably credible material</u>

supporting the allegations. Merely having your client inform you that he/she heard rumours about it does not constitute sufficient grounds for the allegation.

If you have instructions to allege fraud but no evidence, you should maintain your independence and refuse to put the allegations forward.

It must also be noted that even though you can make allegations in Court against a third party without mentioning them by name you cannot do so unless <u>reasonably necessary and </u>you have <u>reasonable grounds</u> for the allegation.

## 6.6 Access to the Judge

There is a fundamental principle that justice should generally take place in open Court. It is normally only allowed to see a Judge in private if it relates to a matter of embarrassment to the client or Counsel or matters regarding your client's safety - assistance to the police- which it is not wished to be made known in open Court.

Judges should not be seen to discuss sentences. Plea-bargaining is not permitted with the Judge. If the client wishes to obtain plead guilty indications about sentence by the Judge, you need to follow the procedure set out in Archbold.

## 6.7 Fee arrangement

You must only propose, or accept, fee arrangements which are legal.

You <u>must</u> make or accept any fee proposal within a reasonable time after receiving the instructions.

It is important to note that you <u>must not receive, control or handle client money</u> apart from what the client pays you for your services unless you are acting in your capacity as the manager of an authorised non-BSB body.

## 6.7.1 Prohibited referral fee

Referral fees either received or paid by yourself or an intermediary is inconsistent with both the obligation to act in the best interest of the client (CD2) to maintain your honesty and integrity (CD3) and to maintain your independence (CD4) and may also breach your duty to not behave in a way which is likely to diminish the trust and confidence which the public places in you or in the profession (CD5).

The BSB will consider a number of features when determining whether a payment to a third party making a referral, acting as an introducer or providing administrative and marketing services constitutes a prohibited referral fee. A payment for these purposes includes not only a financial payment but also any benefits in kind such as the provision of services or facilities for no cost or at a reduced rate.

A prohibited referral fee is:

a)  To make or receive any payment or other consideration,
b)  To or from any intermediary (as defined),
c)  In return for the referral of professional instructions.

Where public funding is in place, the Legal Aid Agency's Unified Contract Standard Terms explicitly prohibit contract-holders from making or receiving any payment (or any other benefit) for the referral or introduction of a client, whether or not the lay client knows of, and consents to the payment. In a private or publicly funded case, a referral fee to which the client has not consented may constitute a bribe and therefore a criminal offence under the Bribery Act 2010.

Referral fees are prohibited where they relate to a claim or potential claim for damages for personal injury or death or arise out of circumstances involving personal injury or death according to the Legal Aid, Sentencing and Punishment of Offenders Act 2012.

Reasonable and genuine expenses that are not rewards for referring work are allowed. These include:

a) Clerking and administrative costs (including outsourcing costs);
b) Membership subscription to ADR bodies that appoint mediators, arbitrators and other adjudicators;
c) Advertising or publicity payable irrespective of whether the work is referred.

It must be noted that a fee which varies depending on the amount of work received does not necessarily mean that it is a referral fee.

The following are likely to be indicators of prohibited referral fee:

a) The payment is made in circumstances which amount to bribery under the Bribery Act 2010;
b) The payment is made in connection with personal injury work and is prohibited by the Legal Aid, Sentencing and Punishment of Offenders Act 2012;
c) The payment is made to a professional person acting for the lay client who has a duty to act in the best interests of that client when making a referral;
d) The payment to an introducer is linked to specific referrals or to the number of referrals;
e) In a publicly funded case, the fee paid to an instructed barrister is less than the Legal Aid Agency fee for those advocacy services;
f) The payment is a condition of receiving a referral;
g) A payment for marketing or related services is higher than market rates;
h) The provision of junior barristers for a fee clearly below the market rate, or below that prescribed by regulation or subject to an

applicable protocol, is capable of amounting to a disguised commission payment.

The following may suggest that the payment is not a referral fee:

a) The payment is made to an employee or agent of the barrister making the payment, e.g. a clerk or an outsourced clerking service, in return for the services they provide to the barrister and not for onward payment to any person who refers work to the barrister;

b) The payment is made to a marketing or advertising agency and the amount does not depend on whether any instructions are received or on the value of any instructions received;

c) The payment is made to an introducer who is not an authorised person or other professional person for the purpose of being included in a list of providers of legal services and the amount is not dependent on the number of referrals received from that introducer.

In considering whether to take enforcement action in cases where payments have been made which may amount to referral fees, the BSB will take a purposive approach and will consider the underlying nature and purpose of the arrangements and whether or not they were in the best interests of clients.

## 6.7.2 Gifts and entertainment

You can never accept money (whether a loan or otherwise), other than your professional fee or reimbursement of expenses or of disbursements made on behalf of the client.

You can however accept other gifts of <u>modest size which would not reasonably be seen as compromising your independence</u>.

If offered a gift by a current or prospective client, professional client or intermediary, you should consider carefully whether the <u>circumstances</u>

PROFESSIONAL ETHICS: A REVISION GUIDE FOR THE BPTC

and the size of the gift would reasonably lead others to think that your independence has been compromised. When assessing the size of the gift you should consider the value of the case. If this is the case you should refuse the gift.

It is important to note that this obligation applies both to receiving gifts and giving gifts to a professional client for instance.

This includes entertainment at a disproportionate level which may give rise to a perception that your independence may be or may have been compromised. You should consider the circumstances and the size of the offer of entertainment. It must be clarified that what amounts to something disproportionate is a grey area but you must not behave in a way which is likely to diminish the trust and confidence which the public places in the profession. While it would not necessarily be improper to accept a lunch invitation, it should not be accepted if it would lead others to reasonably think that your independence has been compromised.

## 6.7.3 Prohibition from holding client money

You must not receive, control or handle client money apart from what the client pays you for your services unless you are acting in your capacity as the manager of an authorised non-BSB body. The prohibition applies to holding client money and other client assets yourself, through an agent, third party or nominee.

Receiving, controlling or handling client money includes entering into any arrangement which gives you de facto control over the use and/or destination of funds provided by or for the client or intended by another party to be transmitted to the client whether or not those funds are beneficially owned by your client and whether or not held in accounts of yours.

This means that if you can cause money to be transferred from the client's account without the client consent it amounts to de facto control.

The client's consent may be deemed to have been given if the client:

a) Has given informed consent to an arrangement which enables withdrawals to be made after the client has received an invoice;

b) Has not objected to the withdrawal within a pre-arranged reasonable period (not less than a week from receipt of the invoice).

It must be noted that a fixed fee is not client money for the purposes of this Rule so handling of a fixed fee would be allowed. However, you may only request an upfront fixed fee if you have estimated accurately the likely time commitment and only take payment when you are satisfied that it is reasonable payment for the work being undertaken.

You must also ensure that it is work that is suitable for you to undertake and whether it is appropriate for you to take the case.

You should always consider a stage payment where the amount of work is unclear rather than a fixed fee. You may also make an arrangement with the client so that you will pay back the difference between the fixed fee and the lower fee earned on the basis of the time spent if lower, as long as you do not hold the balance on trust for the client. The difference will not be client money if you have:

a) An express agreement in writing; which is,

b) based on clear terms understood by the client and concluded before the payment of the fixed fee.

You should also consider whether such an agreement is in the interest of the client bearing in mind the nature of the case, the client and whether he/she understands the implications of such an arrangement.

Any abuse of such agreements will be considered as holding client's money and will be in breach of your duties under the Handbook.

### 6.7.4 Working with a Legal Advice Centre

A barrister <u>must not</u> receive any legal fees from any client of a Legal Advice Centre or any reward for the supply of the work other than a salary paid by the Legal Advice Centre. If any such fees are paid, the barrister must ensure that the fees are paid to:

a) The Legal Advice Centre;
b) The Access to Justice Foundation or
c) Any other Charity prescribed by the Lord Chancellor under the Legal Services Act 2007.

Please also note that a self-employed barrister does not need to inform the BSB that they are also working for a Legal Advice Centre.

## 6.8 Media comments

Another instance which could affect a barrister's independence is the expression of a personal opinion in the media.

Although there is no prohibition on speaking to the media about a case you are involved in, and barristers are free to make comments to or in the media because of the special position they occupy, certain Rules limit the circumstances in which it will be appropriate for barristers to comment on cases in which they have been instructed and what they can properly say. As such, you <u>must</u> exercise good professional judgment in deciding whether or not to comment.

The ethical obligations that apply in relation to your professional practice generally continue to apply in relation to media comment. In particular, barristers should be aware of the following:

a) Client's best interests: Core Duty 2 and the duty to promote fearlessly and by all proper and lawful means the lay client's best interests and to do so without regard to your own interests;

b) Independence: Core Duties 3 and 4 provide that you must not permit your absolute independence, integrity and freedom from external pressures to be compromised;

c) Trust and confidence: you must not diminish the public's trust and confidence in you and the profession, as under CD 5;

d) Confidentiality: under CD 6, you have a duty to preserve the confidentiality of your lay client's affairs and you must not undermine this unless permitted to do so by law or with the express consent of the lay client.

Any comment must not undermine or be reasonably seen as undermining a barrister's independence. In addition, media statements must not bring the profession, nor any other barrister into disrepute.

Special consideration should be taken in cases where media comments have the potential of causing a substantial risk of serious prejudice of current or pending proceedings and may lead to proceedings for contempt of Court.

For instance, a comment which would be a lie would breach CD5, comments which would reveal privileged information or your irrelevant opinion about the strength of the Prosecution case might cause substantial risk of serious prejudice to the proceedings. Similarly, comments that are defamatory would amount to a breach of your duties under the Handbook and may engage your responsibility. Barristers should be aware of the risk of personal liability for claims in defamation or malicious falsehood, or even against the client (if the barrister is speaking on the client's behalf.

The Media Comment Guidance clarifies that among the factors which the barrister should consider when exercising professional judgment about whether and how to comment are the following:

a) The nature and type of proceedings;

b) The stage of the proceedings;

c) The need to ensure that media comment does not prejudice the administration of justice;

d) The nature of the comment that is proposed to be made;
e) The consent of the client if relevant as ill-judged comments on an individual case may cause unintended harm to the interests of the client.

This applies to both conventional media- speaking to newspapers or broadcasters - and new media - social media, blogs and websites. However, comments on a case are allowed in the limited circumstances of an educational or academic context to the extent that no confidential information is disclosed unless authority has been granted by the client.

## 6.9 Criminal Conduct 'other than minor criminal offences'

Any conduct that is a criminal conduct other than a minor offence or constitutes an abuse of professional position may amount to a breach of CD 3 or 5.

A Minor criminal offence includes:

a) An offence committed in the UK which is a fixed penalty offence under the Road Traffic Offenders Act 1988; or
b) An offence committed in the UK or abroad which is dealt by a procedure substantially similar to that of a fixed-penalty offence; or
c) An offence whose main legal element is unlawful; parking of a motor vehicle.

## 6.10 Abuse of professional position, dishonesty and seriously offensive or discreditable conduct

Referring to your status as barrister in a context where it is irrelevant such as in a private dispute may constitute abuse of professional position.

An instance of that could be mentioning your profession and/or your professional influence to impact a situation.

Bar Council Guidance confirms that: "You should not attempt to gain an advantage or put pressure on other people by virtue of your position as a barrister. It would be inappropriate for you to use your status as an implied threat to those with whom you are in dispute. Using Chambers "notepaper in correspondence about a personal dispute, or when conducting personal business, could well constitute an <u>implied threat and leave you open to a justified complaint of professional misconduct</u>. Thought should also be given as to whether the use of an email address identifying Chambers in the context of such a dispute might also contain an implied threat."

This amounts to improper conduct and is likely to diminish the trust and confidence which the public places in the barrister himself or the profession, in breach of CD 5. It also means that the barrister has not acted with honesty and integrity in breach of CD 3.

Any behaviour that is seriously offensive and/or discreditable such as insulting people and/or threatening them would also have the same effect.

Any act which would be fraudulent or deceitful would be dishonest. Dishonesty is a serious misconduct and would amount to a breach of CD3 which needs to be <u>promptly</u> reported to the BSB.

It must also be noted that there is a duty to take all reasonable steps to mitigate the effects of serious misconduct but that even though steps are taken the duty to report still remains.

## 6.11 Discrimination, unlawful victimisation or harassment

You must not discriminate unlawfully against, any other person on the grounds of:

a) Race;
b) Colour;
c) Ethnic or national origin (or nationality);
d) Citizenship;
e) Sex;
f) Gender reassignment;
g) Sexual orientation;
h) Marital or civil partnership status;
i) Disability;
j) Age;
k) Religion or belief;
l) Pregnancy and maternity.

Refusing to provide service, providing service to a lower standard or offering a service on different terms because of any protected characteristic amounts to a breach of the duty not to discriminate.

The Equality Act 2010 contains the duty to make <u>reasonable adjustments</u> where <u>a practice, policy or procedure or physical feature of premises</u> make it <u>impossible or unreasonably difficult</u> for a disabled person to make use of a service. This includes a duty to make auxiliary aids or additional services available such as providing information on audio tapes or a sign language interpreter.

In every situation you must consider what are the reasonable adjustment possible before being able to refuse a case on this basis. In almost every case, spending a greater amount of time on the brief would be a reasonable adjustment and you can therefore not consider that there is no reasonable adjustment possible.

Refusing to make reasonable adjustments amounts to discrimination.

In doing so it is important to note that a barrister cannot pass on the costs of such reasonably adjustments to the individual for whom they are made.

In addition, any act of harassment, defined in the Equality Act 2010 as <u>unwanted conduct</u> that has the <u>purpose or effect </u>of creating an <u>intimidating, hostile, degrading, humiliating or offensive environment</u> for the complainant, or <u>violating the complainant's dignity</u> would amount to a serious misconduct which would breach your duty under CD3 and 4 and entail an obligation to report to the BSB.

## 6.12  Failure to comply with undertakings

Failure to comply with undertakings you give in the course of proceedings may amount to a breach of your Core Duty to conduct yourself with honesty and integrity (CD3) as well as your duty not to behave in a way that is likely to diminish the trust and confidence which the public places in you or in the profession (CD5).

You should ensure that your insurance covers you in respect of any liability incurred in giving an undertaking.

## 6.13  Foreign work

When working in foreign jurisdictions or before international tribunals you <u>must </u>comply with any applicable Rule of conduct prescribed by the law to the national bar where the work is performed or the place where the proceeding take place <u>unless they are inconsistent with the Core Duties.</u>

When engaging in cross border activities within a country of the Council of Bars and Law Societies of Europe you must comply with some Rules of the Code of Conduct for European Lawyers.

# CHAPTER 7

## THE DUTY NOT TO DISCRIMINATE UNLAWFULLY AGAINST ANY PERSON (CD 8)

The Equality and Diversity Rules of the BSB provide that you must take reasonable steps to ensure that your Chambers or BSB authorised body has:

a)  In force a written statement of policy on equality and diversity;
b)  In force a written plan implementing that policy.

In addition, your Chambers must have:

a)  <u>At least one</u> Equality and Diversity Officer responsible for any selection panel;
b)  Training in fair recruitment and selection processes for every member of all selection panels;
c)  <u>Fair and objective</u> recruitment and selection criteria;
d)  Equality monitoring reviews <u>annually</u> conducted on its policy on equality and diversity and of its implementation;
e)  Fair access to work such that there is a fair and equitable distribution of work opportunities among pupils and members of Chambers;
f)  A written anti-harassment policy condemning harassment and putting forward a procedure for complaints and communication of the policy;

g) Parental leave policy giving the right to a member of Chamber to return to Chambers after a specified period (which must be at least one year) of parental or adoption leave during which he/she is not required to contribute to Chambers' rent and expenses as well as a procedure for dealing with complaints;

h) Flexible working hours policy which covers the right of a member of Chambers, manager or employee (as the case may be) to take a career break, to work part-time, to work flexible hours, or to work from home, so as to enable him to manage their family responsibilities or disability without giving up work;

i) Reasonable adjustments policy aimed at supporting disabled clients, its workforce and others including temporary visitors;

j) At least one Diversity Data Officer to comply with the requirements in relation to the collection, processing and publication of diversity data. Details of the Diversity Data Officer to the Bar Standards Board and must notify the Bar Standards Board of any change to the identity of the Diversity Data Officer, as soon as reasonably practicable.

## 7.1 Equality monitoring reviews

The Equality monitoring reviews should include an analysis of the number and percentages of its workforce from different groups, the applications to become a member of its workforce; and in case of Chambers, the allocation of unassigned work. The date should be broken down by race, disability and gender; should investigate the reasons for disparities and take appropriate remedial action.

The Diversity Data Officer shall invite members of the workforce to provide diversity data in respect of themselves using the model questionnaire of the BSB's Supporting Information on the Handbook Equality Rules and shall ensure that such data is anonymized. The data or a summary of it shall be published on Chambers' or BSB authorised body's website every three years. If Chambers or the BSB authorised body does not have a website, the Diversity Data Officer shall make such data available to the public on request.

## 7.2  Sharing work opportunities fairly

The BSB places an obligation on practices to take reasonable steps to ensure the work opportunities are shared fairly among its workforce. In the case of Chambers, this obligation includes work which has not been allocated by the solicitor to a named barrister. It includes fairness in presenting to solicitors names for consideration and fairness in opportunities to attract future named work. These obligations apply even if individual members of Chambers incorporate their practices, or use a "ProcureCo" to obtain or distribute work, as long as their relationship between each other remains one of independent service providers competing for the same work while sharing clerking arrangements and costs.

## 7.3  Harassment

Harassment is defined in the Equality Act 2010 as <u>unwanted conduct</u> that has the <u>purpose or effect </u>of creating an i<u>ntimidating, hostile, degrading, humiliating or offensive environment</u> for the complainant, or <u>violating the complainant's dignity</u>.

Unwanted conduct of a sexual nature would amount to sexual harassment. Treating a person less favourably than another person because they have either submitted to, or did not submit to, sexual harassment or harassment related to sex or gender reassignment.

There is an obligation on all barristers not to victimise anyone for making in good faith a report of serious misconduct. This means that barristers must not treat any individual less favourably because they have made such a report to the BSB.

When making such an assessment you should also take account of the fact that pupil barristers and barristers of fewer years' standing, may be particularly vulnerable due to their relatively junior status within a practice and their relative dependence on more senior barristers for work, guidance and support.

If you are a pupil barrister, or relatively new entrant to the profession, who has become aware of behaviour potentially amounting to serious misconduct, you may wish first to discuss your concerns with relevant colleagues, with your supervisor, the Head of Chambers or HOLP. You may wish to establish whether any other person is aware of the misconduct in question and/or whether that individual is willing to report the misconduct, or has already done so. You do not need to make a report yourself if you reasonably believe that another person has already done so. You can also speak to the BSB or alternatively contact the Bar Council's Ethical Advice line for further assistance.

If the matter relates to conduct which affects you personally, or relates to sexual or other harassment, you still remain under an obligation to report serious misconduct to the BSB. However, the BSB will treat any report of discrimination, harassment (whether of a sexual nature or otherwise), or victimisation as <u>sensitively</u> as possible and <u>will not act without first consulting with any alleged victim</u>.

Given the sensitivity of this issue, the BSB would not ordinarily take disciplinary action if you fail to comply with the duty to report because you believe you are a victim of the misconduct in question. Nevertheless, you should consider the risk that if the matter is not reported, you or others may suffer from similar treatment in the future.

# CHAPTER 8

## THE DUTY TO THE REGULATORS AND OBLIGATIONS OF MANAGERS (CD 9 AND 10)

CD 9 covers the duty to be open and co-operative with your regulators and CD10 the duty to take reasonable steps to manage your practice, or carry out your role within your practice, competently and in such a way as to achieve compliance with your legal and regulatory obligations.

### 8.1  Provision of information to the BSB

Your duties under the Handbook are such that you <u>must:</u>

   a)  <u>Promptly</u> provide all such information to the BSB as it may require <u>for the purpose of its regulatory functions</u> and notify it of any material changes to that information;

   b)  <u>Comply in due time</u> with any decisions or sentence imposed by the BSB, a Disciplinary Tribunal, the High Court or other panel about your fitness to practise.

It must be noted that BSB authorised bodies also have to comply by providing the BSB whatever cooperation is necessary, including to deliver documents to the BSB in connection with your activities.

## 8.2  Obligation to reply promptly

The BSB imposes an obligation to respond promptly to any request from the BSB for comments or information on <u>any matter</u> whether or not the matter relates to you or another BSB regulated person.

## 8.3  Providing privileged information to the BSB

The BSB's request may include access to client information that is subject to legal privilege. As discussed previously, you are <u>not entitled</u> to disclose such information without the consent of the client. You may enquire wither your client is willing to waive privilege. However, you must be aware that you may have a conflict of interest in advising him whether he/she should provide the information or not.

A barrister also has the right to withhold information that is privileged in relation to him and his/her own position from the BSB.

The BSB will consider the issue of privilege on a case by case basis.

## 8.4  Duty to report matters relating to fitness to practice to the BSB

You must report <u>promptly </u>to the BSB if:

a) You are <u>charged</u> with an <u>indictable offence</u> in the jurisdiction of England and Wales or with a criminal offence of comparable seriousness in any other jurisdiction;

b) You are <u>convicted</u> of, or <u>accept a caution</u>, for <u>any criminal offence</u>, in <u>any jurisdiction</u>, other than a minor criminal offence;

c) You (or an entity of which you are a manager) are the subject of any <u>disciplinary or other regulatory or enforcement action</u> by another Approved Regulator or other regulator;

d) You are a <u>registered European lawyer</u> and to your knowledge any investigation into your conduct is commenced by your home regulator, or you are charged with a disciplinary offence, any finding of professional misconduct is made or your professional title is withdrawn or suspended;

e) Bankruptcy proceedings are initiated in respect of or against you;

f) Director's disqualification proceedings are initiated against you;

g) A bankruptcy order or director's disqualification order is made against you;

h) You have made a composition or arrangement with, or granted a trust deed for, your creditors;

i) Winding up proceedings are initiated in respect of or against you;

j) You have had an administrator, administrative receiver, receiver or liquidator appointed in respect of you;

k) Administration proceedings are initiated in respect of or against you;

l) You have committed serious misconduct;

m) You become authorised to practise by another approved regulator.

## 8.4.1 Criminal conduct

Any conduct that is a criminal conduct other than a minor offence or constitutes an abuse of professional position may amount to a breach of CD 3 or 5 and must be reported to the BSB <u>upon being charged</u> (not convicted) and before the conviction/caution is spent irrespective of where the incident or conviction happened.

It must be noted that there is no obligation to report arrest but only being charged.

It is important to note that even a caution for an offence other than a minor criminal offence should be reported to the BSB, but a mere threat of a complaint to the police should not. Fines and other bans such as a ban from driving should also be reported if they result from conviction.

Bankruptcy and other director's disqualification proceedings also go to your credit worthiness and therefore should be reported to the BSB.

### 8.4.2 Serious misconduct

Subject to your duty to keep the affairs of each client confidential, you must report to the BSB if you have reasonable grounds to believe that there has been serious misconduct by yourself, a barrister or a registered European lawyer.

Serious misconduct includes:

a) Dishonesty;
b) Assault;
c) Harassment;
d) Seeking to gain access without consent to instructions or other confidential information relating to the opposing party's case or another member of Chambers, member of staff or pupil;
e) Encouraging a witness to give evidence which is untruthful or misleading;
f) Knowingly or recklessly misleading, or attempting to mislead, the Court or an opponent;
g) Being drunk or under the influence of drugs in Court;
h) Failure by a barrister to report their own misconduct promptly to the Bar Standards Board;
i) A breach by a barrister to comply with obligations to the regulator;
j) Conduct that poses a serious risk to the public.

Whether or not misconduct is serious misconduct is a matter of judgement, which will depend on the particular circumstances according to the Guidance on Reporting Serious Misconduct.

If you are in doubt as to whether or not particular behaviour amounts to serious misconduct you should consider discussing this with the Bar Council's Ethical Enquiries Helpline. It is important to be aware that by reporting what you believe may be serious misconduct simply puts the BSB in a position to decide what action, if any, to take by making a fair assessment as to whether or not serious misconduct (or any misconduct) has in fact occurred. Action will only be taken in relation to the barrister or lawyer concerned where this is <u>appropriate, proportionate and in accordance with the BSB's policies.</u>

It will ultimately be for the BSB to decide whether enforcement action is necessary. If, having considered the factors and circumstance discussed above, you remain unsure whether or not the behaviour in question amounts to serious misconduct, you should <u>err on the side of caution</u> and make a report to the BSB. Issues of competence will not normally constitute serious misconduct unless so serious that it poses a <u>serious risk to the public</u> or would <u>diminish the trust and confidence which the public places in the profession.</u>

It must also be noted that there is a duty to <u>take all reasonable steps to mitigate the effects of serious misconduct</u> but that <u>even though steps are taken the duty to report still remains.</u>

Any other minor misconduct does not need to be reported unless it triggers investigation by a regulator unless <u>it falls short of serious misconduct</u> in which case it should be reported to the HOLP so that they keep a record of the non-compliance.

### 8.4.3 Duty to report serious misconduct of others

If you consider there has been a serious misconduct you should <u>carefully consider:</u>

a) Whether the persons' instructions or other confidential matters might have bearing on the assessment of their conduct;

b) Whether the person has been offered an opportunity to explain their conduct, and if not, why not;

c) Any explanations which has been or could be offered for behaviours;

d) Whether or not the matter has been raised or will be raised in the litigation in which it occurred and if not, why not.

If having given due consideration to the circumstances you have materials which establish a reasonably credible case of serious misconduct you must report it to the BSB. The test is whether you have reasonable grounds to believe that there has been serious misconduct by a barrister or a registered European Lawyer or BSB authorised body, you must report it to the BSB, subject to your duty to keep the affairs of the client confidential.

In case of reporting an opposing Counsel for drunkenness for instance, you should not engage the responsibility of the opposing party for their choice of Counsel or advise them to retain different Counsel.

You must not make or threaten to make a report without a genuine and reasonably held belief that the incident is a serious misconduct. For example, you should not report serious misconduct merely speculatively, out of malice, or to use the reporting of misconduct, or the threat of it, as a 'litigation tactic'. You should only make a report with regard to the Outcomes which the Rule is intended to achieve, described above.

The exceptions to this duty are:

a) If the information is in the public domain and circumstances are such that you reasonably consider it likely that the facts will have come to the attention of the BSB;

b) The conduct has already been reported;

c) The information is subject to legal professional privilege.

In case of professional privilege, you may only disclose the information if the client consents.

The Handbook also includes a protection not to victimise individuals for making good faith reports to the BSB.

## 8.5  Access to premises

You must permit the Bar Council, or the BSB, <u>or any person appointed by them</u>, <u>reasonable access</u>, on request, to inspect:

a) Any premises from which you provide, or are believed to provide, legal services ; and
b) Any documents or records relating to those premises and your practice.

The BSB authorised body, and the Bar Council, Bar Standards Board, or any person appointed by them, shall be entitled to take copies of such documents or records as may be required by them for the purposes of their functions.

## 8.6  Cooperation with Legal Ombudsman

You must give the Legal Ombudsman <u>all reasonable assistance requested</u> of you, in connection with the investigation, consideration, and determination, of complaints made under the Ombudsman scheme.

## 8.7  CD 10 includes obligation to mitigate effects of breach

The obligation to take reasonable steps to manage the practice or carry out your role competently includes an obligation to take <u>all reasonable steps </u>to mitigate the effect of any breach once the BSB regulated person becomes aware of it.

## 8.8 Obligations of Managers

### 8.8.1 Administration of self-employed practice

You must take reasonable steps to ensure that:

a) Your practice is efficiently and properly administered having regard to the nature of your practice;
b) Proper records are kept;
c) Your chamber has appointed an individual to liaise with the BSB in relation to regulatory requirements;
d) Your chamber does not employ disqualified individuals;
e) Proper arrangements are in place to address conflicts of interest and confidentiality of client's affairs;
f) Proper arrangements are in place to deal with pupillages and pupils.

You must not do anything which causes or substantially contributes to a breach of the Handbook by anyone within Chambers. Appropriate risk management procedures must be in place including to ensure all the members of your Chambers have insurance and practicing certificates.

### 8.8.2 Disqualification of non-authorised persons

You also have an obligation to ensure that all the non-authorised persons working in your Chambers are competent to carry out their duties in a correct and efficient manner and are made aware of the provisions of the Handbook which may affect them.

It must be noted that an order can be made by a Disciplinary Tribunal to either indefinitely or for a stated period disqualify a relevant person from one of more relevant activities and prohibiting any BSB authorised person from appointing them or directly or indirectly employing them if they satisfy the disqualification condition.

The disqualification condition means that an employee of a BSB autho-rised body or a HOLP or HOFA has intentionally or through neglect:

a) Breached a relevant duty which the BSB regulated person is sub-ject to under the Handbook or the Rules of another regulator;
b) Caused or substantially contributed to a BSB regulated person breaching a relevant duty under the Handbook or the Rules of another regulator; and
c) In either case it is undesirable for the relevant person to engage in the specific activity.

### 8.8.3 Keeping Records

When deciding how long records need to kept you should take into con-sideration various requirements such as the obligations in the Handbook, under the Data Protection Act and the HM Revenue and Customs.

You must provide the client with such records or details of the work you have done as may reasonably be required for the purposes of verifying your charges.

You must also ensure that adequate records supporting the fees charged or claimed are kept at least until the later of either:

a) Your fees have been paid or;
b) Any determination or assessment of costs in the case has been completed and the time for appeal against assessment or deter-mination has expired or the appeal is complete.

### 8.8.4 Continuing Professional Development requirements

As a manager you should take reasonable steps to ensure that managers and employees within your organisation regularly undertake professional development and educational activities to maintain and develop their competence and performance.

Merely complying with the Continuing Professional Development requirements may not be sufficient to comply with your obligations to provide a competent standard of work.

### 8.8.5 Assignment of work

You should also ensure that work is allocated appropriately to managers and employees with regards to their appropriate knowledge and expertise to undertake such work.

In addition, your personal duty to act in the best interest of the client requires you to assist in the distribution of client files and otherwise assisting to ensure that each client's interests are projected in the event that the BSB authorised body itself is unable to do so in case of insolvency for instance.

### 8.8.6 Third party payment service

In light of the prohibition against holding client money, a third party payment system may be used for making payments to or from your behalf. However, you must ensure that:

a)  The service you use will not result in your receiving, controlling or handling money;
b)  The service is only used for funds in respect of legal services such as fees, disbursements or settlement monies;
c)  The service is authorised or regulated by the Financial Conduct Authority (FCA);
d)  The clients' money must be segregated from the barrister's own funds;

e) The client consent is required for payment;
f) The client is informed that the monies held by the payment service provider are not covered by the Financial Services Compensation Scheme, the service is adequately insured if it is a small payment institution; and
g) You take reasonable steps to check that making use of the service is consistent with your duty to act competently and in your client's best interest.

You must also ensure that the service is not holding client's money as your agent as this will amount to a breach of your duties.

It is important to note that you will be expected to behave as a <u>reasonably competent legal adviser acting in the client's best interest.</u> Unless the service is safe for your client's use you should advise your client against using the third party payment system and you should not use it yourself.

## 8.8.7 Winding down operations

Once you are aware that you (if you are a self-employed barrister or a BSB authorised body) or the BSB authorised body within which you work (if you are an authorised individual or manager of such BSB authorised body) will cease to practise, you shall effect the orderly wind-down of activities, including:

a) Informing the BSB and providing them with a contact address;
b) Notifying those clients for whom you have current matters and liaising with them in respect of the arrangements that they would like to be put in place in respect of those matters;
c) Providing such information to the BSB in respect of your practice and your proposed arrangements in respect of the winding down of your activities as the BSB may require.

## 8.8.8  Advertising

While the Handbook does not prohibit advertising, it must comply with the general provisions of the Handbook and in particular with the duty:

a) Not to mislead clients and potential clients;
b) Of confidentiality to the clients.

A barrister may not publish details of his/her success rates but may publish photographs, rates and charging methods and details of cases which are already publicly available. If the information you wish to use to advertise is in the public domain then you can do so but if you wish to include privileged information you will need to obtain the client's consent first.

## 8.8.9  Associations with others

Where you are in an association on more than a one-off basis you must notify the BSB accordingly and provide the details of the association to the BSB as required. Please also note that the Rules relating to conflict of interest described previously will also be applicable.

You may not use an association to evade Rules which would otherwise apply to you or to do anything which you would otherwise be prohibited from doing.

You must also ensure that the association is not carrying out any illegal activities as you will otherwise bring the profession in disrepute by associating with it and be in breach of your obligations pursuant to the Handbook.

Any interest in an organisation as owner or manger would fall under these rules.

## 8.8.10 Obligation to exclude from Chambers in case of breach

The Constitution of Chambers should allow you to exclude from Chambers a member whose conduct is reasonably considered such as to diminish the trust the public places in you and your profession and you should take such steps as are reasonably available to you to exclude such members unless they accept sanctions taken against them and are not disbarred.

## 8.8.11 Confidentiality obligations of Managers

The Handbook requires barristers to preserve the confidentiality of the client's affairs. Barristers are data controllers under the Data Protection Act and must comply with the requirements of the Act in handling data to which that Act applies. They are responsible for the conduct of those who undertake work on their behalf and are advised to ensure that clerks and other Chambers' staff are aware of the need to handle and dispose of confidential material securely.

Chambers must have appropriate data management systems for looking after confidential information. It must be noted that the obligations of the Handbook relating to the implementation of systems in Chambers applies to tenants in a law firm.

In making arrangements to look after the information entrusted to them, barristers should seek to reduce the risk of casual or deliberate unauthorised access to it. Consideration needs to be given to information kept in electronic form as well as on paper.

The arrangements should cover:

- The handling and storage of confidential information.
- Suitable arrangements should be made for distributing papers and sending faxes and emails.

- Particular care should be taken when using removable devices such as laptops, removable discs, CDs, USB memory sticks and PDAs.
- When no longer required, all confidential material must be disposed of securely, for example by returning it to the client or professional client, shredding paper, permanently erasing information no longer required and securely disposing of any electronic devices which hold confidential information.

Additional safeguards will need to be put in place for particularly sensitive information, or for cases in which Counsel from the same Chambers are appearing on opposing sides.

## 8.8.12 Complaint procedure

In addition to providing such information to clients upon accepting instructions, the Chamber's website must display information about the Chamber's complaints procedure.

You must also ensure that an adequate complaints procedure is in place which includes:

a) Process by which all complaints are acknowledged promptly;
b) That the complainant is provided with:
- The name of the person dealing with the complaint, a description of his/her role in Chambers and contact information;
- A copy of the Chamber's complaints procedure or the BSB authorised body complaints procedure;
- The date by which the complainant will hear back from Chambers.

Once the Chambers has dealt with the complaint the complainant must be told in writing of their right to complain to the Legal Ombudsman and of the time limit.

All the information relating to complaints <u>must</u> be kept confidential and must only be disclosed only so far as is necessary for:

a)   The investigation and resolution of complaints;
b)   Internal review in order to improve Chambers handling of complaints;
c)   Complying with requests from the BSB in monitoring and auditing functions.

However, disclosure to the BSB does not include minutes of meetings to discuss complaints.

A record must also be kept for 6 years from resolution of the complaint of:

a)   Each complaint;
b)   All steps to respond to it (including all correspondences); and
c)   The outcome of the complaint.

The person responsible for the administration of the procedure must also report at least annually to the member of Chambers of the HOLP.


## 8.8.13  Discrimination

There is an obligation to rake reasonable steps to ensure that Chambers has a reasonable adjustment policy aimed at supporting disabled clients, its workforce and others including temporary visitors. Any costs incurred in doing so cannot be passed on to the disabled client.


## 8.8.14  Insurance

You <u>must</u> ensure you have adequate insurance considering the nature of the practice which covers <u>all the legal services you supply to the public.</u> You must respect the minimum limit/terms of insurance set by the BSB.

Any self-employed barrister must be a member of the Bar Mutual (or referred to as the BMIF), with the exception of pupils covered by the pupil master's insurance. As a member of the Bar Mutual you must pay promptly the insurance premium required and supply such information as the BMIF may require from time to time.

A BSB authorised body must confirm annually that it has reviewed the adequacy of its insurance cover on the basis of any risk analysis and has complied with the obligations of the Handbook.

As mentioned previously, the Guidance on Insurance and Limitation of Liability provides that barristers may limit or exclude their liability in ways that are permitted at law.

# CHAPTER 9

## Quality Assurance Scheme for Advocates Rules

QASA is a joint scheme being developed by the BSB, the SRA and CILEx Regulation to regulate the quality of all advocates appearing in the criminal Courts in England and Wales, whether they are barristers, solicitors, or legal executives. The Scheme will apply to all advocates, whether they are self-employed or employed, and whether they are acting for the prosecution or defence.

The Scheme will systematically assess and assure the quality of criminal advocacy in the Courts in England and Wales and will ensure that the performance of all advocates is measured against the same set of standards, regardless of an advocate's previous education and training. The legality of the scheme was challenged before the Courts and found to be lawful and proportionate in June 2015.

You should not undertake criminal advocacy unless you have provisional accreditation or full accreditation in accordance with QASA rules.

## 9.1 Objectives of QASA

QASA has one simple objective, to protect the public from those advocates who are not as good as they should be. This Scheme will ensure the person representing you in the criminal Courts is competent to do their job as incompetent advocacy can lead to miscarriages of justice.

Trained Judges will be encouraged to submit evaluation forms in circum-stances where they have concerns about an advocate's competence. Where a regulator has concerns about an advocate's competence at their existing level, it may send a trained Independent Assessor to assess an advocate in trial. In circumstances where an advocate is found to be acting beyond their competence, the advocate concerned will be moved down a level (and will have to demonstrate competence at their new level).

## 9.2 Stages of assessment

The sorts of competencies advocates will be tested against include their knowledge, preparation, presentation of written and or oral submissions and how they conduct questioning. The Criminal Advocacy Evaluation Form (CAEF) lists the nine competencies and what is expected at each of the levels.

There are three main types of assessment:

a) Registration – in order to enter the scheme once it becomes op-erational, advocates will need to prove their competence at their current level;

b) Progression – advocates will be able to apply to move up a level when they believe they are competent. This will be a two-stage process involving assessment at the current level followed by as-sessment at the new level;

c) Re-accreditation – if an advocate remains at the same level for 5 years, they will need to prove their competence at that level in the fifth year.

## 9.3 No QASA accreditation

Barristers who do not have provisional accreditation or full accredita-tion under the QASA are permitted to undertake criminal advocacy:

a) In hearings which primarily involve advocacy which is outside of the definition of criminal advocacy; or

b) If they have been instructed specifically as a result of their specialism in work outside of the definition of criminal advocacy.

You should only undertake criminal advocacy in hearings which you are satisfied fall within the QASA level at which you are accredited, or any QASA level below the same, unless you are satisfied that you are competent to accept instructions for a case at a higher QASA level strictly in accordance with the criteria prescribed in the QASA Handbook.

## 9.4 Provisional and full accreditation

Any provisional accreditation must be converted into full accreditation within 12 or 24 months of the date when the provisional accreditation was granted.

If you are granted full accreditation, it will be valid for 5 years.

# CHAPTER 10

## THE CODE FOR CROWN PROSECUTORS AND THE FARQUHARSON GUIDELINES

## 10.1 Code for Crown Prosecutors

The Code for Crown Prosecutors sets out the basic principles followed by Crown Prosecutors when they make case decisions on <u>whether or not to charge</u> a case against a suspect. The Full Code Test is applied and has two stages:

a) The evidential stage;
b) The public interest stage.

The Code for Crown Prosecutors states that "Prosecutors must be <u>fair, independent and objective</u>. They must not let any personal views (...) influence their decisions" for both of these stages.

### 10.1.1 The evidential stage

This is the first stage in the decision to prosecute. Crown Prosecutors must be satisfied that there is <u>enough evidence</u> to provide a "<u>realistic prospect of conviction</u>" against <u>each</u> defendant on <u>each</u> charge.

They must consider whether the evidence can be used and is reliable.

They must also consider what the defence case may be and how that is likely to affect the prosecution case.

A "realistic prospect of conviction" is an <u>objective test</u>. It means that a jury or a bench of magistrates, properly directed in accordance with the law, will be more likely than not to convict the defendant of the charge alleged.

If the case does not pass the evidential stage, it must not go ahead, no matter how important or serious it may be.

Whenever considering a decision of a Prosecutor you must consider whether the evidential test has been passed and only after whether the public interest stage is satisfied.

### 10.1.2  The public interest stage

If the case does pass the evidential stage, Crown Prosecutors must then decide whether a prosecution is needed in the public interest. They must balance factors for and against prosecution carefully and fairly.

Some factors may increase the need to prosecute but others may suggest that another course of action would be better. A prosecution will usually take place unless there are public interest factors tending against prosecution which clearly outweigh those tending in favour.

The CPS will only start or continue a prosecution if a case has passed both stages.

## 10.2  Farquharson Guidelines

Farquharson Guidelines provides the Rules for the Prosecution Advocate. Whilst the Guidelines are not legally binding unless expressly approved by the Court of Appeal, they nonetheless provide important practical guidance for practitioners involved in the prosecution process.

## 10.2.1 Pre-Trial

It is the duty of Prosecution Counsel to read the Instructions delivered to him expeditiously by the Crown Prosecution Service (CPS) and to advise or confer with those instructing him on all aspects of the case well before the Court hearing or draft/agree the indictment.

The instructions:

a) address the issues in the case including any strategic decisions that have been or may need to be made;
b) identify relevant case law;
c) explain the basis and rationale of any decision made in relation to the disclosure of unused material;
d) where practical, provide specific guidance or indicate;
e) where a case is an appeal either to the Crown Court from the magistrates' Court or is before the Court of Appeal, Divisional Court or House of Lords, address the issues raised in the Notice of Appeal, Case Stated, Application for Judicial Review or Petition.

On receipt of instructions the Prosecution Advocate will consider the papers and advise the CPS, ordinarily in writing, or orally in cases of urgency if:

a) he/she forms a different view to that expressed by The CPS (or where applicable a previous Prosecution Advocate) on acceptability of plea;
b) the indictment requires amendment;
c) additional evidence is required or there is an evidential deficiency (which cannot be addressed by the obtaining of further evidence) and there is no longer a realistic prospect of conviction;

d) he/she believes that it is not in the public interest to continue the prosecution;
e) certain formal admissions should be made in order to expedite and simplify proceedings;
f) he/she disagrees with a decision that has been made; or is not satisfied that he/she is in possession of all relevant documentation; or considers that he/she or she has not been fully instructed regarding disclosure matters;
g) a case conference is required (particularly where there is a sensitive issue e.g. informant/PII/disclosure etc);
h) parameters on acceptable plea(s) need to be defined; and
i) the presentation of the case to the Court requires special preparation of material for the jury or presentational aids.

The Prosecution Advocate will endeavour to respond within five working days of receiving instructions, or within such period as may be specified or agreed where the case is substantial or the issues complex.

The Prosecution Advocate will inform the CPS without delay where the advocate is unlikely to be available to undertake the prosecution or advise within the relevant timescale.

When a draft case summary is prepared by the CPS, the Prosecution Advocate will consider the summary and either agree the contents or advise the CPS of any proposed amendment.

## 10.2.2  Case Management

On receipt of a Case Management Plan the Prosecution Advocate, having considered the papers, will contact the Crown Prosecutor within seven days, or such period as may be specified or agreed where the case is substantial or the issues complex, to discuss and agree the plan. The plan will be maintained and regularly reviewed to reflect the progress of the case.

The CPS will inform the Prosecution Advocate of developments in the case without delay and, where a decision is required which may materially affect the conduct and presentation of the case, will consult with the Prosecution Advocate prior to that decision.

### 10.2.2.1 Victims and witnesses

When a decision whether or not to prosecute is based on the public interest, the CPS will <u>always consider the consequences of that decision for the victim and will take into account any views expressed by the victim or the victim's family</u>.

### 10.2.2.2 Conduct of the Case

While he/she remains instructed, the Prosecution Advocate takes all necessary decisions in the presentation and general conduct of the prosecution but is subject to the principles and procedures relating to matters of policy.

Until the conclusion of the trial the Prosecution Advocate and CPS have a continuing duty to keep under review decisions regarding disclosure. The Prosecution Advocate should in every case specifically consider whether he/she can satisfactorily discharge the duty of continuing review on the basis of the material supplied already, or whether it is necessary to inspect further material or to reconsider material already inspected. Disclosure <u>must </u>always follow the established law and procedure and unless consultation is impracticable or cannot be achieved without a delay to the hearing, it is desirable that the CPS and, where appropriate, the disclosure officer are consulted over disclosure decisions.

### 10.2.2.3 Policy Decisions

Policy decisions are non-evidential decisions on: the acceptance of pleas of guilty to lesser counts or groups of counts or available alternatives;

offering no evidence on particular counts; consideration of a re-trial; whether to lodge an appeal; certification of a point of law; and the withdrawal of the prosecution as a whole.

Where concerning matters of policy it is the duty of Counsel to consult his/her Instructing Solicitor/Crown Prosecutor whose views at this stage are of crucial importance. In case of disagreement the Prosecution Counsel will make the necessary decisions.

At trial though, the Prosecution Advocate should alert The CPS at the first opportunity if a matter of policy is likely to arise. He/she must not give an indication or undertaking which binds the prosecution without first discussing the issue with the CPS.

At the Crown Court, an experienced Crown Prosecutor will be available at the Crown Court to discuss and agree any issue involving the conduct or progress of the case. When it is not possible to provide a Crown Prosecutor at court, an experienced caseworker will attend and facilitate communication between the Prosecution Advocate and the Crown Prosecutor having responsibility for the case. In exceptional circumstances where it is not possible to contact a Crown Prosecutor, the Prosecution Advocate should ask the Court to adjourn the hearing for a realistic period in order to consult with The CPS. Where an adjournment is refused, the Prosecution Advocate may make the decision but should record his or her reasons in writing.

Where an issue remains unresolved following consultation with a Crown Prosecutor; or where the case/issue under consideration is substantial, sensitive or complex; or the Prosecution Advocate disagrees with the advice of the Crown Prosecutor, the matter may be referred to the Chief Crown Prosecutor, the Director Casework or to a senior Crown Prosecutor with delegated authority to act on their behalf and the Court should be asked to adjourn if necessary. When an adjournment is sought, the facts leading to the application should be placed before the Court only in so far as they are relevant to that application.

Where a Chief Crown Prosecutor has been directly involved in the decision making process and the issue remains unresolved, the matter may be referred to the Director of Public Prosecutions.

In exceptional cases where Counsel has taken a decision on a matter of policy with which his/her Instructing Solicitor has not agreed, then it would be appropriate for the Attorney General to require Counsel to submit to him a written report of all the circumstances, including his/her reasons for disagreeing with those who instruct him. Where, by agreement, the issue remains one that either party considers should be drawn to the attention of the Director of Public Prosecutions, the Prosecution Advocate will, on request, provide a written report for submission to the Director of Public Prosecutions. If he/she considers it appropriate to do so, the Director of Public Prosecutions may refer the matter to the Attorney General.

Where there has been a disagreement on a matter of policy, provided that The CPS is satisfied that the Prosecution Advocate followed the principles set out in this document, the professional codes of conduct and was not Wednesbury unreasonable, The CPS <u>will not apply sanctions in respect of any future work solely as a result of the decision in a particular case.</u>

### 10.2.2.4 *Change of Advice*

When Counsel at the last moment before trial unexpectedly advises that the case should not proceed or that pleas to lesser offences should be accepted, and his/her Instructing Solicitor does not accept such advice, Counsel should apply for an adjournment if instructed so to do. The CPS and the Prosecution Advocate should agree a period of adjournment that would allow a newly instructed advocate to prepare for trial. The period should be realistic and acknowledge that in such circumstances a case conference will usually be required. The facts leading to the application for the adjournment should be placed before the Court only in so far as they are relevant to that application.

### 10.2.2.5 *Disagreements with the CPS*

The CPS will consult and take all reasonable steps to resolve any issue or disagreement and will only consider withdrawing instructions from a Prosecution Advocate as a last resort.

If the Prosecution Advocate disagrees with any part of his/her instructions, the advocate should contact the responsible Crown Prosecutor to discuss the matter. Until the disagreement has been resolved the matter will remain confidential and must not be discussed by the Prosecution Advocate with any other party to the proceedings.

## 10.2.3  Decision-making at trial

It is for Prosecution Counsel to decide whether to offer no evidence on a particular count or on the indictment as a whole and whether to accept pleas to a lesser count or counts. The Prosecution Advocate may ask the Defence Advocate whether a plea will be forthcoming but at this initial stage should not suggest or indicate a plea that might be considered acceptable to the prosecution before a plea is offered.

Where the Defence Advocate subsequently offers details of a plea, the Prosecution Advocate may discuss the matter with a view to establishing an acceptable plea that reflects the defendant's criminality and provides the Court with sufficient powers to sentence appropriately.

Where the Prosecution Advocate forms the view that the appropriate course is to accept a plea before proceedings commence or continue, or to offer no evidence on the indictment or any part of it, the Prosecution Advocate should:

1.  whenever practicable, speak with the victim or victim's family attending Court to explain the position;

2. ensure that <u>the interests of the victim or any views expressed by the victim or victim's family are taken into account</u> as part of the decision making process; and
3. keep the victim or victim's family attending Court informed and explain decisions as they are made.

Even though the Prosecuting Counsel represents the State and not directly the victim, the Counsel is encouraged to keep the complainant informed about what is going on <u>and</u> explain what may happen but <u>does not require the victim's consent</u>. Where appropriate, the Prosecution Advocate may seek an adjournment of the Court hearing in order to facilitate discussion with the victim or victim's family.

The Prosecution Advocate should where practicable, discuss the matter with The CPS before informing the Defence Advocate or the Court that a plea is acceptable. Where the defendant indicates an acceptable plea, unless the issue is simple, the defence should put the plea in writing. The Prosecution Advocate should show The CPS any written record relating to the plea and agree with The CPS the basis on which the case will be opened to the Court.

It is the responsibility of the Prosecution Advocate to ensure that the Defence Advocate is aware of the basis on which the plea is accepted by the prosecution and the way in which the prosecution case will be opened to the Court.

### *10.2.3.1 Sentencing*

The Prosecution Advocate should always draw the Court's attention to any matters, including aggravating or mitigating features that might affect sentence. Additionally, the advocate should be in a position to assist the Court, if requested, with any statutory provisions or sentencing guidelines and should always draw attention to potential sentencing errors.

### 10.2.3.2 Judicial approval

If Prosecution Counsel invites the Judge to approve the course he/she is proposing to take, then he/she must abide by the Judge's decision.

A discussion with the Judge about the acceptability of a plea or conduct of the case should be held in the presence of the defendant unless exceptional circumstances apply such as information which should not be made public or there are sensitivities surrounding a prosecution decision or proposed action which need to be explained in chambers with a view to obtaining judicial approval. Such approval may be given in open Court where it is necessary to explain a prosecution decision or action in order to maintain public confidence in the criminal justice system.

In exceptional circumstances, where the Prosecution Advocate considers it appropriate to communicate with the Judge or seek the Judge's view in Chambers, The CPS should be consulted before such a step is taken. Where discussions take place in Chambers it is the responsibility of the Prosecution Advocate to remind the Judge, if necessary, that an independent record must always be kept. The Prosecution Advocate should also make a full note of such an event, recording all decisions and comments. This note should be made available to The CPS.

If Prosecution Counsel does not invite the Judge's approval of his/her decision it is open to the Judge to express his/her dissent with the course proposed and invite Counsel to reconsider the matter with those instructing him, but having done so, the final decision remains with Counsel. Where a Judge expresses a view based on the evidence or public interest, The CPS will carry out a further review of the case.

The Prosecution Advocate will inform The CPS in a case where the Judge has expressed a dissenting view and will agree the action to be taken. Where there is no CPS representative at Court, the Prosecution Advocate will provide a note of the Judge's comments.

The Prosecution Advocate will ensure that the Judge is aware of all factors that have a bearing on the prosecution decision to adopt a particular course. Where there is a difference of opinion between the Prosecution Advocate and The CPS the Judge will be informed as to the nature of the disagreement.

In an extreme case where the Judge is of the opinion that the course proposed by Counsel would lead to serious injustice, he/she may decline to proceed with the case until Counsel has consulted with either the Director or the Attorney General as may be appropriate.

### 10.2.3.3 Appeals

Where the Prosecution Advocate forms a different view to that expressed by the CPS on the conduct/approach to the appeal, the advocate should advise the CPS <u>within five working days of receiving instructions or such period agreed where the case is substantial or the issues complex</u>.

## 10.3 Returning and withdrawal of instructions

When returning a brief, the advocate originally instructed <u>must ensure that the case is in good order and should discuss outstanding issues or potential difficulties</u> with the advocate receiving the brief.

A solicitor who has briefed Counsel to prosecute <u>may</u> withdraw his/her instructions <u>before the commencement of the trial up to the point when it becomes impracticable to do so,</u> if:

a)   he disagrees with the advice given by Counsel; or
b)   for any other <u>proper professional reason</u>.

The Prosecution Advocate will keep the CPS informed of <u>any personal concerns, reservations or ethical issues </u>that the advocate considers have the potential to lead to possible conflict with his/her instructions. Where the CPS identifies the potential for professional embarrassment or has concerns about the Prosecution Advocate's ability or experience to present the case effectively to the Court, the CPS reserves the right to withdraw instructions.

It is often difficult to define when, in the course of a prosecution, it becomes impracticable to withdraw instructions as circumstances will vary according to the case. The nature of the case, its complexity, witness availability and the view of the Court will often be factors that will influence the decision.

In the majority of prosecutions it will not be practicable to withdraw instructions once the Judge has called the case before the Court as a preliminary step to the swearing of the jury.

If instructions are withdrawn, the Prosecution Advocate will be informed in writing and reasons will be given. Instructions may only be withdrawn by or with the consent of the Chief Crown Prosecutor, Assistant Chief Crown Prosecutor, Head of a CPS Trials Unit or, in appropriate cases, Head of a CPS Criminal Justice Unit or in relation to cases prosecuted by The CPS Casework Directorate, the decision may only be taken by the Director Casework or Head of Division.

# CHAPTER 11

## Disciplinary action

## 11.1 Types of complaints

Complaints are expressions of dissatisfaction by clients. The BSB's Guidance documents on handling complaints draws a distinction between complaints that relate to service, professional negligence and misconduct.

Service complaints are complaints that relate to an act or omission by an authorised person in relation to services provided to the complainant (directly or indirectly) but a single complaint may have elements of all three and the obligations on Chambers are different for each aspect.

Complaints may also have different consequences if they are from clients compared to complaints from non-clients.

### 11.1.1 Complaints about misconduct and professional negligence

It is important to note that Chambers may not always be best placed to seek to resolve or provide redress for complaints which relate to misconduct or professional negligence and there is no positive obligation of Chambers to investigate matters of misconduct.

However, it is likely that in many cases a complaint which raises issues relating to professional misconduct or professional negligence will also amount to an accusation of the provision of poor service or will include a service element. Where this is the case, it is not acceptable for Chambers not to investigate <u>elements of a complaint which relate to service</u> because the complaint also amounts to, or includes elements which relate to, misconduct or could potentially give rise to a <u>negligence claim</u>.

Complainants should be informed <u>in writing</u> if any aspects of their complaint are deemed to be outside of Chambers' complaints handling procedures. This should include information on how to complain to the Legal Ombudsman.

### 11.1.2 Complaints from non-clients

However, the Legal Ombudsman will only deal with complaints from consumers of lawyers' services. This means that only complaints from the barrister's clients fall within the Ombudsman's jurisdiction.

Some non-client complaints, such as discourtesy, may be capable of resolution by Chambers. However, the BSB recognises that Chambers' ability to resolve many kinds of non-client complaints is limited and that they are more suited to consideration under the disciplinary processes of the Bar Standards Board. Accordingly, if Chambers feel that the issues raised by non-clients cannot be satisfactorily resolved through the Chambers complaints process they should refer the complainant to the Bar Standards Board.

## 11.2 Notifying the client of the right to complain

Barristers must notify clients <u>in writing at the time of engagement</u> or if not practicable <u>at the next appropriate opportunity</u>:

a) Of their right to make a complaint, to whom, and how this can be done, including their right to complain to the Legal Ombudsman at the conclusion of the complaints process, the timeframe for doing so and the full details of how to contact the Legal Ombudsman; and

b) That the lay client may complain directly to Chambers without going through solicitors.

This obligation can be satisfied by a letter or e-mail sent directly to the client which may be sent by someone else on his/her behalf providing the required information. If the information has not been provided beforehand in writing, it may be provided on the first occasion that the barrister meets the client at Court, or in conference.

It is important to note that it is not acceptable for barristers simply to make the information available to solicitors. Nor is it sufficient that the information is available on Chambers' website. There is a _positive obligation on the barrister to provide it to the client_.

An _unequivocal agreement_ by the professional client to pass on Chambers' complaint information to the client, either in a particular case, or in relation to each case in which a member of Chambers is instructed by that professional client, will serve to discharge the obligation to provide the client with the information. However, there _must_ be a _positive agreement_ on the part of the professional client: silence is not sufficient.

Where Chambers receive high volume instructions from a particular professional client it will not be necessary to obtain written confirmation in relation to each instruction. In those circumstances, _positive written confirmation_ should be obtained _at regular and reasonable intervals_ from the professional client that complaints information continues to be passed on to lay clients.

Furthermore, there are areas of practice, and particular cases, where it is not possible or practical for the barrister to satisfy the notification requirement in this way. For example, the barrister may not have the contact details of the client, cannot readily obtain them, and does not anticipate meeting the client in the course of being instructed or at least not for some time. In such cases, the BSB prescribes that the barristers use <u>common sense</u> to set up procedures so as fulfil the notification requirements. For example, where a barrister acts for government departments or public bodies it should be possible to agree a standing arrangement with treasury solicitors or other in-house lawyers whereby details of the complaints system is provided to the professional client to be passed on to the client body. Most barristers will be able to think of examples within their own field of practice where procedures can be responsibly adopted so as to fulfil the notification requirement.

Where there are <u>no realistic alternatives to compliance,</u> barristers can provide the requisite information to the solicitor or other professional client with instructions to provide that information to the client on be-half of the barrister, even when the solicitor has not expressly agreed to do so. But this course should only be adopted when other better means of compliance are not practical.

It must be noted that there also exists an obligation to inform at the con-clusion of the complaints process. The complainants must be <u>informed in writing</u> of their right to complain to the Legal Ombudsman.


## 11.2.1  Complaints to Chambers

When a client makes a complaint to Chambers in the first instance, the 14. The Legal Services Board (LSB) seeks to ensure consumers have confidence that:

a)  complaint handling procedures provide effective safeguards for them; and
b)  complaints will be dealt with comprehensively and swiftly, with appropriate redress where necessary.

Chambers complaint handling processes must be convenient and easy to use in particular for those that are vulnerable or have disabilities. They should make provision for complaints to be made by any reasonable means.

The way in which complaints are dealt with <u>must</u> be <u>transparent and clear</u> in relation to process, <u>well publicised and free</u>. In addition, the process itself should be <u>prompt and fair</u>, with decisions based on a <u>sufficient</u> investigation of the circumstances. Where appropriate, there should be an offer of a suitable remedy.

All conversations and documents shall be confidential and disclosed only to the extent necessary. They may be disclosed only to the client, the person complained about, the Head of Chambers, the head of the complaints panel or relevant senior member of the panel, the nominated individual, the management and any other individual with whom enquiries need to be made for the purpose of the investigation.

There is also an obligation to keep records as discussed previously.

The Chambers complaints file should be inspected regularly by the management committee. Papers should be anonymised where necessary. The person responsible for the administration of the system should report at least annually to such appropriate committee of Chambers on the number of complaints received and the subject area of the complaints. In such a report all the details should be anonymised, but should be reviewed for trends and possible training issues.

The BSB will audit and monitor Chambers complaints handling, including, where appropriate, the sufficiency of training. All barristers must comply promptly with requests for information from the committees of the Bar Standards Board dealing with monitoring and auditing.

Most consumers will be able to make a complaint to the Legal Ombudsman about the services they received after they have exhausted Chambers complaints processes. Sufficient information must be provided to all clients to identify whether they do have a right to take their complaint to the Legal Ombudsman and to contact the Legal Ombudsman directly to clarify whether they can.

## 11.2.2 The Legal Ombudsman

The Legal Ombudsman was created by the LSA as an impartial and independent service with the jurisdiction to resolve all client complaints about the services provided by legal professionals and provide redress such as compensation, return of fees, or requiring a legal professional to apologise where appropriate. The LSA removed from all the Approved Regulators of legal services the ability to deal with clients' complaints about service and also the ability to award redress.

The Legal Ombudsman has no powers to deal with complaints of conduct or take disciplinary action against legal professionals and can only address other complaints relating to the provision of the services by legal professionals. It is under a statutory obligation to refer any issues of conduct arising from complaints to the BSB.

In relation to service complaints, the Legal Ombudsman has a range of statutory powers to address them but its aim is to deal with most complaints by informal dispute resolution mechanism.

Legal Ombudsman's website sets out a list of the categories of complaint which it investigates which include the following categories which may also include aspects of negligence or misconduct:

- Costs information deficient
- Costs excessive
- Delay
- Unreasonably refused a service to a complainant

- Persistently or unreasonably offered a service that the complainant does not want
- Failure to advise
- Failure to comply with agreed remedy
- Failure to follow instructions
- Failure to investigate complaint internally
- Failure to keep complainant informed of progress
- Failure to keep papers safe
- Failure to progress complainant's case
- Failure to release files or papers
- Failure to reply
- Misconduct and Professional Negligence

The Legal Ombudsman has the power to make formal directions which are binding on barristers and can be enforced through the Courts including directing barristers to:

- apologise to the complainant;
- limit fees to a specific amount (which may involve return of fees in whole or in part or waiving the right to recover fees);
- pay compensation to the complainant;
- rectify any consequences of poor service at their own expense;
- take any action at their own expense which is in the interests of the complainant. The total amount that be can be directed as an aggregate is £50,000 but interest can also be ordered.

The Legal Ombudsman complaints mechanism has time limits in which a complaint must be raised:

a) Six years from the date of the act/omission;
b) Three years from the date that the complainant should <u>reasonably have known there were grounds for complaint</u> (if the act/omission took place before the 6 October 2010 or was more than six years ago);

c) Within six months of the complainant receiving a <u>final</u> response from their lawyer, if the response included an explanation that the Legal Ombudsman complaints procedure was available if the complainant remained dissatisfied and provided full contact details for the Ombudsman and a warning that the complaint must be referred to them within six months.

The Ombudsman can extend the time limit in exceptional circumstances. Chambers must therefore have regard to that timeframe when deciding whether they are able to investigate your complaint. Chambers will not therefore usually deal with complaints that fall outside of the Legal Ombudsman's time limits.

### 11.2.3 Indemnity insurance

You should ensure that your insurance covers you in respect of any liability incurred in giving an undertaking and for any type of work you perform. Where a complaint raises an allegation of negligence it may be appropriate to inform BMIF and to consult them before any proposals for resolution are made to the client.

## 11.3 Responding to complaints

Whenever you are made aware of the dissatisfaction of a client you should tell him that he/she has a right to complain and that in the first instance the complaint should be made to chambers.

The client should be told that he/she can call the person in Chambers designated to deal with complaints. If the complaints is not resolved during the phone call to Chambers he/she will be invited to put his/her complaint in writing so that it may be investigated normally. He/she will then be sent a copy of the Chambers' complaint procedure if this was not already sent to him.

Alternatively if he/she prefers he/she can make a complaint in writing in which case a copy of the Chambers' complaint procedure should be sent to him.

He should also be informed of the Legal Ombudsman complaint procedure.

You should also tell him that the Chamber's website has a copy of the complaints procedure and inform him of the time limits for the procedure.

Chambers should not charge clients for dealing with their complaint. To do so brings the Bar into disrepute and could amount to professional misconduct.

## 11.4 Threshold of BSB pursuing disciplinary action

Disciplinary proceedings may be taken against a BSB regulated person if the Bar Standards Board believes there has been a breach by that person of the Core Duties set out in the Handbook <u>and</u> that such action would be in accordance with the Enforcement Policy.

In case of reports of serious misconduct, the BSB will decide what action, if any, to take by making a fair assessment as to whether or not serious misconduct (or any misconduct) has in fact occurred. Action will only be taken in relation to the barrister or lawyer concerned where this is <u>appropriate, proportionate and in accordance with the BSB's policies</u>.

## 11.5 Personal responsibility

It is important to note that BSB regulated individuals are personally responsible for their own conduct and for their professional work.

You must use your professional judgment to meet your obligations at all times in relation to the matters on which you are instructed and be able to justify your decisions and actions. You must do this notwithstanding the views of your client, professional client, employer or any other person.

You remain responsible for any work delegated or outsourced and are responsible for the services provided by all those who represent you in your dealings with your clients or any other employees, pupils or agents. You cannot blame pupils for mistakes they have made or blame the tight time schedules as you should have returned the instructions if the work could not be done in the stipulated time.

Even though in terms of civil liability a BSB authorised body can stipulate it in terms and conditions that the body will be responsible for any civil liability incurred by the BSB regulated person, this does not affect the regulatory obligations to which the BSB regulated person is subjected to for professional judgments made.

In some cases, barristers may be liable personally such as for claims in defamation or malicious falsehood, or even against the client if the barrister is speaking on the client's behalf.

It must be noted that a barrister who breaches the Cab Rank Rule will be subject to disciplinary proceedings but will not be liable in the civil Courts. As such, the judiciary have confirmed that it is not a matter for Courts in *Geveran Trading Co Ltd v Skjevesland* [2003] 1 WLR 912 at [42] per Arden LJ.

## 11.6  Personal responsibility of professional client or other individuals

Where a professional client or other individuals providing services to the client has failed to act in the best interest of the client, a barrister is under an obligation to advise the client accordingly.

This includes advising the client about potential disciplinary action against the professional client if any and in relation to damages.

## 11.7  Indemnity insurance

You should ensure that your insurance covers you in respect of any liability incurred in giving an undertaking and for any type of work you perform. Where a complaint raises an allegation of negligence it may be appropriate to inform BMIF and to consult them before any proposals for resolution are made to the client.

## 11.8  Independence of members of Chambers

It must be noted that members in Chambers are not in partnership but are independent from each other and as such are not responsible for the conduct of other members. Each member is responsible for his/her own conduct and the constitution of Chambers should enable each individual member to take steps to terminate another's membership in specified circumstances.

However, you are not required to sever the connections with a member of Chambers solely because to your knowledge he/she has breached his/her obligations pursuant to the Handbook, as long as he/she is not disbarred and complies with sanctions imposed for the breach.

The Constitution of Chambers should allow you to exclude from Chambers a member whose conduct is reasonably considered such as to diminish the trust the public places in you and your profession and you should take such steps as are reasonably available to you to exclude such members.

## 11.9 The Court's power to discipline Counsels

A barrister is under a duty to avoid unnecessary expense or waste of the Court's time. In case of <u>improper, unreasonable or negligent</u> conduct the Court can make wasted costs orders.

Serious misconduct before the Court will usually be apparent to the Judge, and in such cases, the Judge hearing the matter may bring the serious misconduct to the Head of Chambers and in more serious cases to the Bar Council for disciplinary action.

If you are a barrister acting in a judicial capacity, your conduct <u>duties as a Judge take precedence over your professional duties as a barrister</u>. The BSB would not expect to take enforcement action against a barrister acting in a judicial capacity.

Whilst the obligation to report does not impact on a barrister sitting in a judicial capacity, nothing in this guidance should be taken as preventing barristers from reporting to the regulator serious misconduct observed by a barrister, when sitting, in the normal way.

## 11.10 Academic misconduct for students on the BPTC

Finally, a student found guilty by their course provider of cheating or other misconduct on the BPTC course amounts to a <u>serious matter</u> and the Inn's Conduct Committee may:

a) Advise the student as to future conduct;
b) Reprimand the student;
c) Order that the student's call to the Bar be postponed for a specified period;
d) Expel the student from the Inn.

Printed in Great Britain
by Amazon